PEA'S LADIES

Rose Hamilton-Gottlieb

Culicidae Press, LLC
PO Box 5069
Madison, WI 53705-5069
culicidaepress.com
editor@culicidaepress.com

Ames | Berlin | Lemgo

PEA'S LADIES
Copyright © 2024 by Rose Hamilton-Gottlieb
All rights reserved.

No part of this book may be reproduced in any form by any electronic or mechanized means (including photocopying, recording, or information storage and retrieval) without written permission, except in the case of brief quotations embodied in critical articles and reviews. For more information, please visit culicidaepress.com

ISBN: 978-1-68315-090-9

Library of Congress Control Number: 2024936997

Our books may be purchased in bulk for promotional, educational or business use. Please contact your local bookseller or the Culicidae Press Sales Department at +1-515-462-0278 or by email at sales@culicidaepress.com

twitter.com/culicidaepress – facebook.com/culicidaepress
threads.net/@culicidaepress – instagram.com/culicidaepress

Design by polytekton © 2024
Cover images generated by Midjourney AI system and modified by polytekton

For my writer friends, in California and Iowa.

Contents

Chapter One	6
Chapter Two	8
Chapter Three	15
Chapter Four	22
Chapter Five	26
Chapter Six	31
Chapter Seven	34
Chapter Eight	38
Chapter Nine	43
Chapter Ten	47
Chapter Eleven	50
Chapter Twelve	54
Chapter Thirteen	61
Chapter Fourteen	66
Chapter Fifteen	72
Chapter Sixteen	75
Chapter Seventeen	77
Chapter Eighteen	79
Chapter Nineteen	82
Chapter Twenty	86
Chapter Twenty-One	89

Chapter Twenty-Two	91
Chapter Twenty-Three	96
Chapter Twenty-Four	99
Chapter Twenty-Five	105
Chapter Twenty-Six	108
Chapter Twenty-Seven	111
Chapter Twenty-Eight	113
Chapter Twenty-Nine	116
Chapter Thirty	124
Chapter Thirty-One	127
Chapter Thirty-Two	129
Chapter Thirty-Three	132
Epilogue	141

Chapter One

Pea was reading his morning paper and having his coffee with one teaspoon of cream and two lumps of sugar when Maizie leaned on his doorbell and hollered through the open door of his basement apartment. Why hadn't he closed that door? He could have pretended he hadn't heard Maizie's shrill call, although in truth he would have heard her with the door and all the windows shut tight. Even in bed with a pillow over his head. When Maizie Dillard wanted to be heard, she was heard.

On this beautiful morning, rare for February in Maryland, with the sun warming the brick sidewalk in front of Hobarth Manor and melting the last bit of snow, Pea McNulty emerged from his snug, caretaker's apartment at the side of the building to where Maizie waited on the sidewalk, letter in hand.

"Have you seen this?" She thrust it at him, nearly knocking him off balance. "If I read this correctly, we have five months to vacate this building. You notice it doesn't say three months to find a new home. No, it says, 'vacate the building.' As if all that matters is Hobarth Manor be emptied of us. Of me and Fiona and Carlotta and Sulie and Nan. And you, too, I imagine, Pea. If three months from this day the owners showed up, they'd be satisfied, I suppose, to see us all sitting on our steamer trunks on the sidewalks. Having vacated."

While Maizie went on, Pea scanned the letter. Shock waves moved from the back of his head and down through his untied sneakers into the warm bricks of the sidewalk. He wondered, distractedly, why his trembling didn't cause an earthquake.

Maizie, however, seemed to have no trouble holding her ground, as her center of gravity was much lower than Pea's. She had wide hips and muscled arms, covered this morning with a dark green sweater, well pilled, with a snag on the collar and the corner of one pocket unstitched. Her thick glasses rested on a thin nose. Her sparse grey hair was carelessly chopped off above the ears with a few scraggly bangs falling forward.

Pea handed back the letter, trying to appear calm. For wasn't it his job to create a secure environment for his ladies? To protect them from outside disturbances, from excessive noise, cold, and heat? To keep the pipes flowing and the newspapers delivered outside their doors and their windows to the outside world clean and unstuck? Hadn't he cared for them for almost as long as he could remember? While he reflected on this, Maizie stood impatiently before him.

"So. You didn't know then." Her voice revealed both satisfaction for being the first to know, and panic that Pea had not stood between her and this news.

Chapter Two

Early the next day, Pea dressed in his best suit and hat and set out. He turned at the end of the brick walk to study the building, admiring his favorite aspect of the facade: thirty-six ladies in flowing gowns, two on each side of eighteen windows. He couldn't have told anyone they were caryatids; he could only say they bestowed a grace and calm to the only home he'd ever known.

Hobarth Manor had an elegance from another time, when Baltimore was the settling place for several families of Italian stonemasons. The portico was supported by fluted marble columns. Above, *Hobarth Manor* was carved in bas relief and underscored by a vine-leaf frieze. Above that was a Palladian window, its three large panes looking out from a sitting area on the upper floor. Over all were more vines and colored fruit. Light reflected off the marble facade, and light poured into the spacious apartments through the many windows, which continued, without the caryatids, on all four sides of the building, with two side-bay windows at either end of the long central hallway. It was a building of light.

On this morning in particular, Pea felt a sense of proprietorship. By rights Hobarth Manor was his, for who else cared for it the way he did? He'd been born in the basement apartment where his caretaker parents had lived. He'd played in the park across the street and walked to school. He took the streetcar downtown to work in a garage where he learned to fix things. He left only to fight in Korea, returning home to his widowed mother. He cared for her and for the building, which gradually became the last line of defense for a succession of elderly couples. Now, in his late fifties, he felt responsible for the aging apartment building and its handful of old ladies.

Pea sighed deeply, vaguely conscious he'd been doing a lot of that for a long time. Turning up his collar against the chill and plunging his hands into the pockets of his father's hound's-tooth overcoat, he set out for the bus stop.

This morning he'd realized his paycheck was late. A review of his checkbook and an upending of the drawer in which he sometimes tossed his uncashed earnings revealed he hadn't received his last three paychecks. He'd been unaware of this because he sometimes waited several months before making a deposit. Pea's needs were modest and most of his salary went into a savings account, or for little extras, such as plantings for the flowerbeds.

Every month for over fifty years, first his father, then his widowed mother, then Pea, had received a check, on time, from Myers and Myers Associates, the owners of Hobarth Manor. Now, it seemed they'd forgotten about him. They'd even neglected to send him an eviction notice, as if he didn't exist. He would see about that.

On his way to catch the 10:15 bus downtown, he passed the Art and Music Institute. Its brick exterior had been sandblasted and a Maryland Historical Trust sign planted on the front lawn. A small bronze plaque listed the famous musicians and artists who had studied there during its hundred-year history. The plaque added stature to the building, as though it had thrown its shoulders back with pride, as parents do at praise of their successful children.

Pea rarely had occasion to go downtown, and as the bus wound through his neighborhood, he was amazed at the changes taking place. Many of the Victorian painted ladies had been torn down, after suffering fifty years or more of the indignities that went with being used and abused as apartment houses. A few had been restored and some of those boasted Maryland Historical Trust signs. Others had been replaced with ugly, compact apartment houses, or with equally ugly one-story buildings. An animal hospital. A hair salon. Several law offices. Perhaps, he mused, a lawyer was what was needed to protect the rights of himself and his ladies. But what, exactly, were their rights?

Pea found the office of Myers and Myers Associates, noting that the door now said Myers, Myers, and Fox Associates. He pondered the name change and why the name 'Fox' rang a bell. He was about to knock when the door opened and a woman burst out, nearly throwing him off balance. "Oh," she said, breathlessly. "Oh my. Please excuse me." A slight woman with stringy brown hair streaked with grey, she ducked her head and hurried off. Pea thought distractedly that there was something familiar about her.

"Come in, if you're coming in," a gruff voice commanded. "And close the door. Heating oil doesn't come out of the faucets, you know." The man behind the desk in the outer office was on the telephone. He didn't look up.

Pea removed his hat and ran his fingers through his sparse hair. He stood on one foot, then the other, before spotting a large street map of Baltimore on the wall. He consulted a key that listed points of interest to find the Art Institute. Hobarth Manor and the park across the street from it were two blocks away. It was oddly comforting to see the old building's location on the map, as if that indicated permanency. From the map he went on to a gallery of photographs, which included a portrait of old man Myers, whom Pea remembered fondly, and his son, less familiar to him, but who nonetheless had signed Pea's paychecks all these years. Next to them was a photo of two men shaking hands. He recognized the older of the two as Walker Knolls, a local politician who frequently had his picture in the paper.

At the sound of the phone receiver being put back in its place, Pea turned to see the man gesture impatiently toward a swivel chair. He sat down, balancing his hat on his knee. The chair had been adjusted so only his toes reached the floor. Feeling like a child, he picked nervously at his hatband.

"State your business if you have any worth stating," the man said. He fixed Pea with an insolent stare. He didn't introduce himself, but the nameplate on the desk read Tod Ryan. Pea ignored his crude manner, but found it impossible to ignore the large mole on the man's cheek. He glanced at the man's hand. No wedding ring. He thought so. A wife surely would have trimmed those three hairs growing out of that mole. And where was Mr. Myers?

"I'm Pea...that is, Percival Jamieson McNulty." His full name felt rusty on his tongue. It was many years since he became "Peanut McNulty," courtesy of an uncle who re-named him because of his small, round-shouldered frame, beige complexion, and pale brown hair, now streaked with grey.

"What can I do for you, Percy?" The man glanced pointedly at his watch.

Pea squared his shoulders. "I'm the caretaker of Hobarth Manor," he said.

The man scowled. "Caretaker? I wasn't aware…"

"Uh…is Mr. Myers in?" Pea said, with a glance toward the closed door of the inner office.

"Mr. Fox is in charge of things now and he hired me to manage the property."

Fox. Why was that name so familiar?

The man shuffled through the piles of papers on his desk. "There's no McNulty on this list of tenants," he said. He consulted a ledger and narrowed his eyes. "And no record of a McNulty having paid any rent."

"That's easily explained, Mr., ah, Ryan," Pea said mildly, with a hesitant glance at the nameplate. "I don't pay rent. In fact, I'm on the payroll. Have been for the past thirty years." He shifted his weight forward in the chair in an attempt to plant his feet firmly on the floor. He cleared his throat, hoping for a deeper register. "Which brings me to one reason for this visit." He hadn't planned on bringing up the issue, at least not right off, but it seemed he had no choice. "I haven't received my last three paychecks."

Mr. Ryan leaned back, his eyes not sharing the smile playing about his mouth. "I have no knowledge of a caretaker at Hobarth Manor. Indeed, the idea is ludicrous. An old relic like that…"

Pea had to bite his tongue not to tell the man how Mr. Myers had readily paid for repairs over the years, no questions asked. He relaxed his clenched fists and took a moment before answering. "Sir," he said stiffly, "have you been to Hobarth Manor?" It was true there were some vacant apartments, but he kept them ready for new tenants. When someone moved out, he painted the walls himself and polished the fine hardwood floors, refinishing whenever necessary, such as the time Sadie was carried off by her daughters to a nursing home and he discovered her toy poodle's water dish had left a milky island in a corner of the kitchen.

"I've seen that monstrosity," Mr. Ryan said. "It not only gives architecture a bad name; it's the most inefficient use of space I've seen in thirty years in the building business." He rose and crossed the room and stabbed the map with a thick finger. "An old half-empty apartment building in an area undergoing gentrification lends itself to two possibilities. One is renovation, bringing it up to standard so it appeals to the right kind of people…"

"And that would be?" Pea demanded. Conscious of his dangling legs, he swiveled his chair to face the map.

"Why, the kind who can afford to pay the prevailing rent, of course. Now the other option, and the only one in this case, is to tear the place down and start from scratch. Put up one of those fake Victorian jobs with three times as many units…"

"At three times the rent," Pea murmured hopelessly. He saw his ladies put out on the sidewalk, Carlotta's piano propped incongruously on the curb, while the wrecking ball demolished the graceful marble figures standing guard over each apartment. Whatever this gentrification was, it didn't sound very gentlemanly.

"Exactly." Mr. Ryan returned to his desk. "Which brings me back to the subject at hand. Now if you're living there, rent-free…"

"I was born there, sir," Pea said. "Except for the time I spent in Korea, I've lived in that basement for fifty-eight years."

"Sleeping in the basement, eh?" The man looked him up and down.

Pea was suddenly conscious that his suit, which had been his father's Sunday best, was shiny at the elbows and smelled of mothballs. Perhaps this man took him for a poor homeless veteran who had climbed in a broken basement window and was making his bed on a pile of dirty rags, like a mouse coming in from the cold. He might as well be a mouse for all his effectiveness. He tried one more time. "Mr. Myers never told you about me?" he said hoarsely. "He never said how I keep the furnace and the elevator in repair and wash the windows? And, by the way, there are vacancies, all ready for new tenants. For some time now, actually. I believe I informed Mr. Myers of that."

"Perhaps you didn't understand," Mr. Ryan said, standing in a posture of dismissal. "There will be no new tenants. And I was told nothing about you."

Pea got up in a daze. Never to be mentioned by Mr. Myers, whose father had come in person every month to play a round of cribbage with Pea's father and have a piece of his mother's sour-cream raisin pie, which he always said he could get nowhere else, for his wife didn't like raisins, and restaurants in general didn't know what was good. Old Mr. Myers died when Pea was in high school, but all these years, his son had faithfully signed the caretaker's paychecks.

Then Pea remembered. He took out his wallet of alligator skin so worn his father's initials were barely visible. Inside, he found a check, which he unfolded and held out so the man could see the signature, *William T. Myers*. "My last paycheck," Pea said triumphantly.

Mr. Ryan glanced at the signature and shrugged. "So, you were on Myers's payroll. For doing the occasional odd job, I suppose. The man who signed that check is dead. I'm dealing with the trustee for his estate. You'd better start looking for another basement to squat in, my friend. That mother is going to come down like a house of cards."

Chapter Three

The emergency meeting of the Tenant's Association was set for 3:00 p.m., after naptime and well before the dinner hour. At exactly 2:45, the strains of Mozart drifted through Carlotta's open door into the sunny upstairs hall. This was the tenants' cue to enter her living room, where framed playbills decorated the walls, and shelves overflowed with music books. Carlotta, dressed in a black crepe gown that had seen better days, sat at the grand piano. Even with arthritic fingers, it was clear she was a pro. She sat perfectly straight, her black hair pulled back in a bun, emphasizing her widow's peak.

One by one, four tenants drifted in, found their assigned seat on dining room chairs, removing name cards printed in Fiona's calligraphy. One chair, with Nan's name on the card, remained vacant. Although she had stopped coming to the meetings, Pea had insisted there always be a chair for her, in the hope she would show up. He especially wanted her there for this meeting.

Maizie, wearing a stained blouse and a mustard-colored wool skirt smelling of mothballs, sat on the far left. She lived on the first floor with Leonardo, her alleged pet alligator, a flagrant violation of the rules, which she always claimed did not apply in her case. The lease she had signed, over thirty years ago, ruled out dogs and cats and all other varieties of creatures with four legs and hair and potentially polluting systems of elimination. Alligators, she claimed, were not named and had never been added to the list. In her opinion, they belonged to the same category as goldfish, which were allowed.

Sulie arrived dressed in red plaid trousers with a green sweater coat. Her white hair was cut in an uneven pageboy. She sat on the other end, as far away from Maizie as possible, an arrangement tactfully initiated by Fiona some years before when Sulie lost control during a discussion and pinched Maizie on the arm. Another reason, Pea thought, for assigned seats. Impatient for the meeting to begin, Sulie twisted a man's handkerchief in hands permanently reddened by years of restaurant work.

Fiona settled next to Maizie. She wore a vintage cream-colored wool suit with pale grey pinstripes, a wide collar, and padded shoulders. The cut of the jacket showed off her small waist. Her heart-shaped face was framed by dyed black hair arranged in finger waves. Her kid gloves matched her navy shoes. She held a leather-bound notebook in which to record the minutes. Most pages held only the date and the names of those present.

Pea sat between Sulie and Nan's vacant chair, dreading what he knew would be his role in this meeting. They would, of course, look to him for some kind of reassurance, and worse, leadership. How could he tell them Hobarth Manor was to be torn down? And how would his ladies face life without him? Who would watch to make sure they had awakened each morning? Who would check to see if they ate more than crackers and tea for supper? And there was Nan's empty chair on his left. Who would guard his favorite tenant's privacy without letting on they knew her secret?

Carlotta finished her piece to polite applause, swiveled on the piano stool and inclined her head in a manner incongruent with the pink crocheted slippers peeking out from the folds of her skirt. "Thank you," she said. "Your adulation is all the reward I require." This was an oblique reference to a petition circulated by the tenants twenty years ago requesting that she restrict her playing to between nine and ten in the morning and three and four in the afternoon, thereby ruining her chance at a comeback to the concert circuit.

As hostess, it fell to Carlotta to open the meeting. "As you know," she began, "I have lived here the longest, except for Pea, of course, who was born here." She nodded graciously in his direction, and he smiled his encouragement. Carlotta had a habit of reciting key aspects of her personal history during their meetings, something he usually found tedious. Today he was grateful for the time it might buy him. He fixed her with an attentive gaze and concentrated on the unseasonably warm air bringing the scent of half-composted leaves from the park across the street.

His mind, usually agile in response to the constant stream of feminine emergencies, was now completely devoid of ideas. In fact, for the last day and a half, he had holed up in his apartment. Maizie had brought him strong tea. Undrinkable, but he appreciated the thought. Sulie carried down a tureen of canned turtle soup, apologizing that it wasn't the real thing, made from her own recipe. Her long-gone restaurant, the renowned Snapper Stew in downtown Baltimore, had been famous for it. Pea didn't care much for turtle soup, but he had no trouble putting away Nan's chocolate layer cake, sent down with the boy who delivered her groceries.

Carlotta held up her copy of the eviction notice. "It seems we're about to lose our home." A general sigh rose from the assemblage. The dreaded subject was on the table and the temptation was for everyone to speak at once. This was forestalled when Carlotta raised one long forefinger. "As you know, my dear Spencer and I moved in when Hobarth Manor was considered *the* address in Rosemont, which was then the fashionable suburb of Baltimore. In those days, there was a red-uniformed door man stationed at the portico, and the chandelier in the entry had all its crystals cleaned monthly." Carlotta gave Pea an apologetic forgiving glance. After all, how could he be expected to clean it more than once or twice a year?

"But I digress," she said, with a glance to discourage Maizie from telling her to get on with it. "If only Spencer were here now, to guide us through this." Again, there was a general intake of breath, and Carlotta again raised her forefinger.

"You all may or may not recall," she went on, "that I met my dear Spencer while on tour at the Lovelett Opera House in Rosemont. He came backstage after the concert, his arms filled with daffodils. How he knew that was my favorite flower is still a mystery to me, but I took it as an omen." She sighed deeply. "I didn't realize, young as I was and full of romantic notions, that the onset of true love sounded the death knell for what promised to be a brilliant career." She paused for effect, ignoring Maizie's smirk. Before she could continue, the shrill sound of a timer filled the room.

Some years ago, to cut down on everyone talking at once, they had agreed that before any general discussion, each one could have the floor for five minutes. Otherwise, by the time grievances were aired and arguments played out, there was often no time for the business at hand, if anyone remembered why the meeting was called in the first place.

Now, Sulie pulled the timer from her sweater pocket and made a show of turning it off. Like the pro she was, Carlotta inclined her head as if the sound of the alarm had been applause. "Very well," she said magnanimously, "I yield the floor to Maizie."

Maizie had her own copy of the letter, which she defiantly crumpled into a ball and tossed onto the coffee table. It landed in the plate of cookies sent over by Nan. "Three months. We've got three months. What am I supposed to do about Leonardo?"

A cautious exchange of glances drifted through the semi-circle. None of the ladies had ever actually seen Leonardo and they doubted his existence. However, there was that occasional splashing sound and the scummy pond smell that came from her spare bathroom whenever she hosted a meeting.

"We'll think of something, Maizie," Pea said. Under the guise of reaching for a cookie, he removed Maizie's crumpled eviction notice and stuck it in his pocket. At least now he had a copy for himself.

"Perhaps your daughter could take Leonardo," Sulie said with exaggerated sweetness.

"That ungrateful one," Maizie muttered. "I send her to college with poor Albert's insurance money to study psychology, and what does she do? She tells me I'm a "toxic personality.""

To everyone's relief, the timer went off again. "That wasn't five minutes," Maizie said. "You always cut me short."

Sulie ignored her while rewinding the timer. "Fiona's turn," she said with an innocent glance at Maizie. In the absence of support from the others, Maizie folded her arms and clamped her mouth shut.

Fiona spoke. "In the interest of moving things forward, I yield my time." This came as no surprise because Fiona rarely had anything to say. If asked about her past, she would smile politely and gaze off into the distance. The only thing she consistently volunteered was her age, shaving nine years off her seventy-nine, thus laying claim to being the youngest of the ladies. Which she was, in any case, except for Nan, who was only seventy but kept it to herself to humor Fiona. At eighty-five, Maizie had seniority.

Each lady had her own theory about Fiona's past. Sulie speculated that she'd been a prostitute on the waterfront, rescued by a lovesick and gullible merchant who showered her with clothes and jewelry. The romantic Carlotta theorized that Fiona's aristocratic bearing suggested she was one of a remnant of European royalty, hiding out from would-be assassins. Maizie suspected her of being a fugitive from the underworld. Pea didn't care about Fiona's past. She rarely presented him with a problem and her self-possession had a calming influence.

"I, too, will skip my turn," Sulie said. "After all," she said, with a reproachful glance at Maizie and Carlotta, "we do have an emergency on our hands."

"Very well," Carlotta said. "Pea, what shall we do?"

They looked at him, and he looked at each in turn, unexpected anger building at their dependence on him, but really at himself for letting them down. Finally, Sulie spoke. "I've been thinking, why do the new owners want us out? We're all good tenants. We pay our rent on time."

"And dear Pea keeps the building in tiptop shape," Carlotta said.

Fiona shook her head. "But how long has it been since our beloved Sadie was carried out on a stretcher? Or since Beatrice expired in her sleep, God rest her soul. Why are their apartments still empty?"

"How many empties are there, Pea?" Maizie demanded.

"Four," he said. "Two on both floors." He'd been secretly glad when Mr. Myers had failed to rent them. Now he could see this wasn't at all in their favor.

"They're going to tear down the place," Sulie said, torturing her handkerchief, "They're going to throw us all out on the street and build a parking lot."

There it was, on the table without his having to say it. He cleared his throat. "I'm afraid I have been informed they are going to tear down Hobarth Manor."

They stared at him. He would have preferred weeping and wailing, anything but this silence he felt obliged to fill. "I can see how to some it would make sense," he began, lamely. Of course, it made no sense at all, but at least it shocked them into speech, momentarily getting him off the hook.

They all spoke at once. "What do you mean? Look at that woodwork"…"those hardwood floors"…"the molding"…"the lovely marble statues in front"…"the brass railing in the elevator that Pea keeps polished…"

Pea was moved by the litany of praise and gratified that they didn't take the building and its unique charms for granted. Nevertheless, to restore order, he lifted the timer from Sulie's lap and set it off. "Now, one at a time," he said, avoiding Sulie's shocked gaze as he pocketed the timer.

"Perhaps you misunderstood, Pea," Carlotta said. "Maybe they plan to renovate the building. Or convert it to condominiums."

"That doesn't help us," Sulie wailed. "We, or at least I, could never afford to buy one."

"They'll sell them at exorbitant prices. To Arabs," Maizie said darkly.

"Arabs?" Sulie said, looking puzzled.

Maizie gave her a withering glance. "It's all over the news. They're buying up everything. Oil money," she added conspiratorially.

"There's only one thing to do," Fiona said. They all turned to the one tenant who always had the least to say. "We have to stick together." It was clear from the silence, and the tentative glances exchanged, that none of them, Pea included, had the slightest idea what that might mean.

Chapter Four

Pea took his usual place at Nan's breakfast table while she poured him a cup of hot chocolate and set before him a plate of cinnamon cookies, still warm from the oven and filling the room with a homey fresh-baked smell. She wore a smock made from an orange and yellow floral print. He recognized the fabric. He'd picked it out for her at K-Mart.

Pea marveled at how Nan had managed to keep her pretty face as the pounds went on. Except for an excessive number of chins, her classic looks, with high cheekbones and well-defined eyebrows, were mostly intact. As she sat across from him, he heard a slight squeak and made a mental note to check the stability of her kitchen chairs.

He took a cookie and pushed the plate toward her.

"Oh no," she demurred. "I couldn't. Too many calories."

Pea nodded. Nan never ate in his presence. Now, as always, she merely sipped a cup of tea. He might wonder how she could keep gaining weight on a diet of green tea, if not for the bags of groceries she had delivered to her door. When the elevator wasn't working, the bags were left in the foyer and Pea's bell would ring, signaling him to carry them up. When that happened, he couldn't help but notice the quantities of sugar and flour and butter and baking chocolate, not to mention the slabs of cheese and jars of peanut butter and jelly and bags of pasta. Someone was consuming all that and as far as Pea knew, he was her only visitor.

When he had eaten his fill, Nan pulled the letter about the eviction notice from her pocket and spread it out on the table. It looked worn. Pea's heart turned over at the thought of her sitting alone, reading and re-reading it. He should have come to her sooner.

"What will I do, Pea? Where am I to go?" she said. "I have no one."

Pea followed her gaze about the spotless, sunny kitchen. Nan's apartment had more light than any of the others, with skylights in every room and tall windows swathed in filmy drapes. She had originally chosen it for its potential as an artist's studio, and her walls held many of what had once been her trademark views of Chesapeake Bay. It had been years, however, since Pea had delivered any art supplies.

A large tear forged a pathway down one powdered cheek, then another, then Nan was sobbing. Mascara began to rim her beautiful eyes. Pea dusted crumbs from his fingers and covered her plump hands with his own. "I really needed you at yesterday's meeting," he said. "Please come to the next one."

She shook her head. "I can't."

A year ago, Nan had sworn she'd never attend another Tenant's Association meeting, declaring she was tired of the airs the other ladies put on and she couldn't take another recitation of their life histories, stories of operations, and complaints about ungrateful children. He hadn't believed her for a minute. Everything she said about the others went against what he knew of her patient nature. However, he'd accepted her voting proxy without comment.

"We really need you this time, Nan," he said. "We need your clear mind and your creativity." Over the years, Nan had been the one tenant he could turn to in times of crisis. She was always fair-minded, never distracted by grievances, real or imagined.

Flustered at the unexpected praise, Nan broke off half a cookie and stuffed it into her mouth. Then, with a blush, she put the remaining half down and covered it with a napkin. "I can't come to a meeting, Pea," she sobbed through a mouthful of crumbs.

"Dear Nan, what is it?" Pea said softly.

"I...I...oh, just look at me. I can't go out anymore. I know it's hard to believe but I used to be beautiful. I can't bear the way people look at me now. And I can't get into anything but these... these tents I run up on my sewing machine."

"But you're still beautiful," Pea blurted out, astonished she didn't realize that.

It was as if he'd never spoken. Her shoulders shook and her chair squeaked in rhythm to her sobs, filling Pea with alarm. "Perhaps there's something that can be done," he said helplessly.

"You're going to tell me to diet," she said — misery and an uncharacteristic, hard resentment creeping into her voice.

"No, no, no," he said, sweeping the idea aside with a gesture of his rough worker's hands, although it was the only solution that came to mind. "Look, Nan, we don't need to talk about that today. Right now, we have to deal with this." He pointed to the letter.

To his relief, Nan stopped crying and wiped her eyes, smearing a napkin with mascara and leaving a black swath on her smooth complexion. Seeing this, Pea rose to his feet and wet a paper towel at the sink and gently wiped away the wayward mascara, tears, the residue of face powder matted on her cheeks, and finally a spray of cookie crumbs from around her mouth.

"Oh Pea," she said, showing every indication of clouding over again.

Nearly moved to tears himself at his own gentle impulse and at the tender feelings she aroused in him, Pea patted her shoulder clumsily and retook his chair. "You'll just have to have the meeting here, Nan," he said firmly. How could he make her realize how much he needed her?

"With me like this?" The panic in her face told him it was no use, and he wondered when she had turned the corner from being the large woman who carried her own weight with style to this shapeless recluse with swollen ankles. Dressed in smocks made from fabric which she maybe wouldn't have chosen for herself, but always accepted without complaint.

"Very well, then, Nan," he said hastily. "But I trust you to do your very best thinking to come up with something, because, because…" What he said next was so difficult he knew she was the only person in the world to whom he could say it. Even then, he could barely get the words out. "I…I need your help." He tapped the letter with a fingernail, feeling more alone than he'd ever felt. "Because this is one thing I cannot fix."

Chapter Five

That night, Pea's dreams were filled with the sound of a wrecking ball crashing into the building while his mother and Nan and even old Mr. Myers called out, "Pea, do something." He awoke bathed in sweat. He'd always been able to do something. Any little thing that went wrong at Hobarth Manor had a solution. Even Nan's predicament must have a solution, existing as it did, in her imagination. But this time the problem wasn't coming from the pipes or the roof. Or from any of the tenants. This was a problem from the dimly understood world of business and finance, and he didn't know his way around that terrain.

When the clock on his bedside table showed 5:00 a.m., his usual rising time, he turned it face down and pulled the covers over his head. And while he slept, his dreams mixed up the past with the present, confusing his parents and others from his childhood with his ladies and Mr. Ryan. Finally, around 9:00 a.m., Pea sat up in bed and pronounced to the-sun-dappled room: "Lacy. Lacy Myers." The woman he'd seen leaving Mr. Ryan's office. The mousy, furtive, injured soul whose eyes had briefly raked his face before she ducked her head and hurried off. Little Lacy with the curls and the teasing laugh.

When he was a boy, Lacy had tagged along with her grandfather, and while the old man played cribbage with Pea's father, ate his mother's raisin cream pie, and pocketed rent checks, the two children went to the park. When it rained, they played Chinese checkers in his mother's sewing room. Pea always let her win. She outgrew him around the age of twelve. He saw her only once more, in a photograph his mother clipped from the society page. Her engagement picture. Not long after that, the Korean War happened to him.

His head filled with cotton from his long sleep, he carried a cup of strong coffee to his mother's desk just inside the storage room. In a deep drawer, he sorted through a hodgepodge of old playbills, his school report cards, a record of his childhood immunizations, a few loose photographs, and obituaries. And near the bottom, a manila folder of newspaper clippings. There, sandwiched between one about the Orioles winning the pennant and a recipe for pumpkin cheesecake, he found it: Lacy's wedding picture. Her pretty face wore the same teasing look he remembered. Beside her stood a younger version of the man he'd seen in the photograph the day before, chumming it up with that politician. Lacy's husband. Was he responsible for the furtive, scurrying manner so unlike the Lacy of his childhood?

He went back to the announcement. "Mr. and Mrs. Harrison Myers of Baltimore proudly announce the engagement of their daughter, Lucinda Adriane Myers, to Bertram Fox III, son of…" He skipped to the part where the happy couple planned to reside at 613 Washburn Avenue. He underlined the address, then consulted the phone book and was surprised to find her number listed. He jotted it down on the clipping. He would call her and offer his condolences for her father's death and maybe he'd find out why Hobarth Manor was slated to come to such an end.

Lacy Fox. Foxy Lacy. How she had liked to play tricks on him. Half-melted chocolate slipped into his back pocket. A cricket in a box beneath his pillow. Three extra aces slipped into a deck of cards. The woman who almost ran him over at the landlord's office looked as if she could use an extra ace or two.

He propped the clipping against the salt and pepper shakers on his breakfast table. While he finished off three thick slices of buttered toast made from Nan's homemade bread, he studied the photograph, yellowed and brittle, of his childhood love. He wondered if the day his mother had shown it to him, his future was secured. Until then the world had seemed open to him, for Lacy, although absent throughout his adolescence, had lived on in his imagination.

Pea wandered back to the bedroom. He was born in the four-poster bed with the walls painted the color of sunshine and his mother's colorful hooked rugs on the blue painted concrete floor. It had been a good life, a reasonably happy one, but it was over. Clinging to it now led in one direction, back to bed with the covers pulled over his head. He helped himself to a third cup of coffee and took stock. He'd saved almost all his earnings over the years. Add that to the small nest egg left by his parents, he supposed he was, by some standards, comfortable. And there was always a place for someone with skills, his father had been fond of saying. He had skills. He would help his ladies find new places. He was incapable, for the moment, of considering Nan's situation, Carlotta's grand piano, and Leonardo. But he would get his ladies settled. Then he'd be free of them. He felt a small guilty thrill.

As he dressed in his usual work pants and sweatshirt, his eye caught the suit he'd flung over the back of a chair the night before. He started to hang it up, but remembering how he'd felt in it during yesterday's interview, he folded it neatly and set it aside for the Goodwill. It was time he had his own good suit to hang in the closet, even if he never had another occasion to wear it. Perhaps Fiona, with her sense of style, would help him pick one out.

He looked again at the newspaper clipping, then put it on a shelf just inside the door to the storeroom, under a framed photograph of his parents. He was moving on, and Lacy Myers belonged in his past. He marched, wearing his resolve like the new suit still in his future, up the steps and out into the late morning sunshine. He went down the street, past the park, and headed for the Seven-Eleven on the corner. He'd buy all the local papers, then go to a coffee shop nearby where he could read the want ads undisturbed.

Having made his decision, Pea felt almost enthusiastic about starting a new life. If fear competed with excitement, he supposed that was only to be expected. But midway down the block, he stopped short. On the lawn of a newly refurbished painted lady was a sign, 'Save Hobarth Manor'.

Forgetting his newspapers, Pea continued around the block. There was a 'Save Hobarth Manor' sign on the lawn of every restored home. Who was responsible? It had to be one of his ladies. But which one had the audacity to do such a thing? Maizie, for one, but even if she had the diplomacy to ask permission of the homeowners to post the signs, her bad knees wouldn't get her this far. Carlotta might think of it, but she seldom followed through with her intentions. Sulie was physically capable but lacked imagination. Nan, of course, was above suspicion. Carlotta, then? Yes, of all his ladies, she had the most outside connections. But how did she manage it with her arthritis?

It was noon when Pea realized he'd taken a circular path back to the sidewalk in front of Hobarth Manor. Could it be saved? Did it deserve to be saved, or was it a monstrosity, as Mr. Ryan claimed? To him it was beautiful, but what did he know? He respected the opinions of experts. Was Mr. Ryan an expert? He was in the business, but he didn't look like someone whose taste could be trusted.

At sight of the first sign, all thoughts of a new life had fled. But wait. What if someone was playing a cruel joke? What could it matter to anyone in the outside world whether or not Hobarth Manor survived? Someone powerful had deemed the property worth more without the old building, and who could stand up against that? His inclination to call another meeting of the Tenant's

Association to question the ladies evaporated. He went out again in search of his newspapers.

Back home, the want ads yielded up half a dozen studio apartments. What more did he need but a place to sleep and cook simple meals? Oatmeal for breakfast, a sandwich for lunch, and a little boiled chicken or grilled fish for his supper. He'd miss Fiona's tuna casseroles and Nan's baked goods. He would even miss Sulie's mock turtle soup, always delivered with an apology that it wasn't the real thing, but, she'd say, "Where on earth could one find fresh snapper these days?" She'd wonder why she even bothered, for according to her, it didn't at all resemble the real thing.

He'd adjust. Pea felt a strange mixture of dismay, abandonment, and guilty liberation when he contemplated life without his ladies. But change, he supposed, was a fact of life, and one he'd mostly been shielded from until now.

Chapter Six

Pea entered his childhood bedroom, now a storage room, and edged his way down a narrow pathway past old chairs, a television stand, a couple dozen radios, Carlotta's old turntable, a succession of empty aquariums outgrown by Leonardo, and his old roller skates, which he fished out of a wicker hamper. These, at least, along with the aquariums, he could throw out. Also, his father's suit. Setting the skates outside the door gave him a solid feeling of accomplishment. He'd begun to clear things out.

Turning back to the room, he spotted a set of kitchen chairs abandoned by a former tenant. He removed a cardboard box smelling of mothballs from one of the chairs and tested its legs. Yes, these would do fine. He would take them up to Nan, one by one, on the pretext of giving her 'loaners' while he repaired those spindly matchsticks she was risking her life on.

That decided, he tackled the box. It contained his army dress uniform and underneath, his picture. His mother had kept the photograph on the table in the front hall, proud, he supposed, at the transformation wrought by the uniform. After all, he'd never been one to win prizes in school. He knew he was a good son, but he'd never been much to brag about, so he allowed her that small pleasure. After her funeral, he stored it away.

And here were his discharge papers. Honorable, the papers said, and he supposed he earned that with his short stint of combat duty and all the creamed beef on toast he'd served up, the pots he'd scrubbed, and all the potatoes he'd peeled. Doing work chosen as punishment for others, and grateful for it.

Pea tried to never think about the war, which had interrupted a life that before and after arranged itself by routine. Not that there hadn't been ample routine in the army. That was the one thing he hadn't minded about it. There was never any doubt what was expected of him, and he wasn't afraid of hard work or deprivation or even disparaging references to his size. Or later, to his character.

He did what he was told, and he'd been lucky. Except for that one time, when he had to do what the army trained him to do. There was no anger in it, nor any sense of right or wrong, just the pulling of a trigger and then watching a life drain away, a part of himself draining off with it. That was it, no horror or remorse or regret, just a leak having sprung somewhere inside he could never quite describe with any degree of accuracy. Not to the chaplain who sat with him after, or to his commanding officer, who threatened a court marshal if he didn't pick up his gun again.

There were, of course, men who got out by being conscientious objectors. It was too late for that, and anyway, he wasn't one. If the President thought it necessary for him to go to war, then he couldn't argue. It was a simple matter of having sprung a leak, and Pea knew if he had to kill again, there would be more leakage until there was nothing left. What then, he couldn't imagine. In the end, because the chaplain liked him and his commanding officer was weary of him, he got to work in the kitchen. If anyone thought him a coward, well, he supposed it was true enough, but soldiers needed to eat, and someone had to clean up their messes. He got by, and he came home.

His mother's clothing was still in the closet. His heart swelled at the bulges in her good navy shoes, conformed to the shape of her bunions. Why hadn't he sorted all this out years ago? And how had he allowed all this other stuff to accumulate? He dumped his mother's shoes in a grocery bag. That didn't seem right, somehow, so he took them out and put them back in the closet, alongside her gray mules with the scarlet poppies on the toes. He'd ask Carlotta and Sulie to give him a hand with his mother's things. He felt better, then, as if that decision represented progress.

The box containing his military artifacts blocked the doorway. He picked it up with the intention of sticking it in a corner. But why keep it? It was a perfectly good uniform, and the picture was nicely framed. Was that reason enough? He'd kept it all these years, out of respect, he supposed, for his mother. But when he thought about moving it into a new home, he felt unaccountably low. He retrieved the discharge papers for safekeeping and placed the box, with the rest of its contents, alongside his father's suit and his roller skates.

He closed the door to the storeroom and went back to the classified ads. There, in the middle of the 'for rent' column, in a box set off in bold lines, was the command: "To P. Meet me tomorrow by the sea at three. I'll save thee and perhaps thee will save me." He let the paper drop, then picked it up again. Had he misread the ad? Could it be? The flutter in his stomach said it was. A message from Lacy.

Chapter Seven

The next morning Pea woke early and sprang out of bed as eagerly as his fifty-eight-year-old springs would allow, the verse from the want ad running through his head. How had Lacy known he would see it? But then she'd always had a sixth sense about things. And she'd be aware of the threat to Hobarth Manor, connected as it was to memories of her grandfather. Apparently to memories of him, as well.

Suddenly it seemed like yesterday when twelve-year-old Lacy had run away from home to tell him her grandfather had died, and her parents were moving to another part of the city. Too far away for her to visit, even if her mother would've let her.

They had escaped to their special place in the park, and she had cried, rubbing her eyes with her fists like a small child. He'd loved her as she mourned the loss of her grandfather who'd kept her by his side as long as he could. She cried also for the loss of Pea and the park and Hobarth Manor itself. "Nothing else is near so much fun," she sobbed. In the end, she clung to his neck, and he felt her damp eyelashes along his chin and her soft lips in the hollow of his neck. When she was gone, he cursed himself for not kissing her and for not even thinking of it until it was too late.

Perhaps if he'd kissed Lacy then, something would have been settled between them. Instead, he simply walked her to the streetcar, not even holding her hand, and said goodbye. Only later, away from the glare of her emotions, he realized something stupendous had happened to him. He's suffered a great loss, never to be restored.

He spent the morning cleaning and polishing the four kitchen chairs, then called to alert Nan he was bringing them up. At her door, he was greeted with the smell of fresh-baked oatmeal cookies.

"I brought you some strong chairs," he said, immediately regretting the oblique reference to her weight. He hoped she wasn't offended, but she smiled and told him how thoughtful he was and how she was getting tired of those old chairs, anyway. Pea exchanged the chairs, noting that the legs on two of the old ones were ready to give way.

While Nan moved about the kitchen, brewing coffee and filling a plate with cookies, Pea wondered when he'd last really looked at her. Why hadn't he noticed how her bulk filled the space between the counter and the island where the cookies were cooling? And when had she last worn anything but the shapeless smocks she ran up on her sewing machine? He eyed the door to her apartment. Just how big was she? How big could she get?

Nan poured the coffee and sat down across from him.

"Uh, Nan," he stammered, "When exactly was the last time you went out?"

She stirred cream into her coffee and looked at him with an expression that said, "Why do you ask?"

"What I mean is, don't you get tired of staying in? Wouldn't it do you good to get out once in awhile?"

"After dark, you mean?" Her tone was bitter, not at all like his Nan.

He steeled himself to go on. "In a few months you'll have to move," he began, but when he saw she was on the verge of tears, his courage melted. He reached for a cookie. She got up and moved

35

to the island, surprising him, as usual, with just how light she was on her feet.

"I'm going to send these cookies home with you," she said. "And you tell the others I'll be happy to bake more for their next meeting." She turned and smiled brightly, her old self once more. "As for having to move, I just know you'll think of something, Pea."

He left Nan's apartment laden down with a loaf of fresh bread and two dozen oatmeal cookies. As far as he could determine, she had saved none for herself. He would eat all of it before the week was out, and not weigh an ounce more, which was one of life's great mysteries, if not to say, unfair.

Back home, he shaved carefully, nicking himself only once on the neck where it didn't really show, trimmed the hairs from his nose and ears, and cleaned his fingernails. He chose a yellow v-neck sweater with only a couple of snags and pulled it over his one white shirt. He considered one of his father's wide neckties, but decided that would be going too far, not to mention uncomfortable.

Outside, Carlotta was waiting for him. With the exception of Maizie, none of his ladies liked to ring his doorbell. They preferred to wait at the top of the steps or on the little stone bench, pretending to sun themselves or to read while they waited in ambush. They knew his habits and usually didn't have to wait long. Only when the weather was bad did they telephone, except for Nan, of course, and she called only when she had something to give him. In fact, her clear sweet voice on the telephone never failed to stimulate his taste buds and set his mouth to watering.

Today, Carlotta was wearing a heavy, moth-eaten coat, although it wasn't all that cold for February. "Oh Pea," she said, looking up from her copy of *Musicians Daily*, as if he were the last person she expected to see.

"What's on your mind, Carlotta?" he asked. Did she intend to confess she was the one behind the 'Save Hobarth Manor' signs?

"This," she said. She drew from between the pages of her magazine a flyer, printed in block letters and bordered in black, which read, "We are sad to announce the impending demise of one of our neighborhood's premier establishments, Hobarth Manor. This prime example of the work of the renowned architect, Oscar Carthington, is about to fall to the most contagious disease of a generally unhealthy society; that is, greed." The last word was enlarged and colored in a muddy purple. The text continued: "Anyone interested in saving this local treasure, please come to a meeting at the Art Institute on Sunday, February 12, at 2:00 p.m." Signed, "The Committee for the Preservation of Hobarth Manor."

"I picked this up at my usual Tuesday meeting of *Pianists at Large* at the Art Institute. And I counted half a dozen 'Save Hobarth Manor' signs on my way there and back. What do you make of all this, Pea? Who is this committee? Do you think they've got a chance? I don't imagine so. Could it be a joke? It's not funny. I've never even heard of Oscar Carthington, this famous architect. Have you? Is he famous like Frank Lloyd Wright? No, I don't suppose so. If he were, I would have heard his name at least. But still, he must be well-known in more learned circles; that is, circles of people learned in architecture." Carlotta could carry on a conversation all by herself for some time, taking two parts—or if necessary, more, for complicated issues. Pea waited patiently for her to wind down, then asked for the flyer.

"Oh, this is for you, Pea. I picked up one for everyone here and one for every mailbox between here and the Institute. We're all going to the meeting, except for Nan, who seemed embarrassed when I called on her. She didn't invite me in; in fact, I don't know when she's opened the door all the way for anyone, has she for you, Pea? I suppose not. Anyway, she said she couldn't make it and when has she last gone out? Is she ill? No, I think not. She looks quite… robust. She paused and Pea took advantage of the gap in the flow of speech to make his departure, flyer in hand. If Carlotta wasn't behind the signs, who was?

Chapter Eight

Pea found Lacy at their old meeting place, a big flat rock, deep in the park. Perching on the edge of the rock, her short legs dangling, she seemed more the little girl than the beautiful bride in the yellowed newspaper, or the wasted matron he ran into earlier in the week. A ball cap covered her ponytail, and she wore jeans and a wool plaid shirt, which she hugged to her chest. She smiled. "I knew you'd show up, Pea. Do they still call you that?"

He nodded around the lump in his throat and climbed up beside her, his own feet dangling only slightly lower than hers. She shivered in the weak February sun. He wished he'd worn a jacket so he could wrap it around her shoulders. "We haven't grown much," he said.

"No, but we got a lot older."

He noticed now how her gray eyes were set off by dark circles.

"You didn't recognize me the other day," she said.

"I did, later. I'm sorry about your father. I never met him in person, but he always dealt fairly with me."

"Unlike my husband. He's the executor of my father's estate. I want you to know, Pea, if I had any say, Hobarth Manor would stay just as it is as long as you could take care of it."

It occurred to Pea that she must have put up the signs. And if she did, she must be behind the flyers as well. It would be like her to invent a fake committee.

"But why don't you have a say, Lacy? Aren't you your father's heir?"

"Yes, but he left everything in Bertie's hands," she said bitterly.

"But how can that be?"

"I have headaches." She grasped either side of her head as if to keep it from flying off. "Terrible headaches. The medication I'm on works, sort of, but it makes me woozy, so I try not to take it. And panic attacks. A couple of years ago, I spent a few days in the psychiatric ward and Bertie convinced Father that for my own good, he should be named trustee. I don't think father realized how ruthless my husband can be."

"Can't you go to court?" Pea wished he knew something about such things.

"I tried. But I need a doctor to testify I'm capable and a judge who doesn't play golf with Bertie."

"Your husband has that kind of power?"

"Yes. No. Oh, I don't know. Influence, yes. And I wouldn't put it past that sanctimonious old coot who signed the papers…" She stopped and pressed her fingers to her temples. Her nails had been bitten to the quick. Her breath became slow and measured. "I mustn't get upset," she whispered.

Pea pulled the flyer from his pocket. He didn't want to upset her, but he had to know. "Uh, do you know anything about this? And the signs posted around the neighborhood?"

"Don't worry, Pea. I was in my right mind when I did that. More or less, anyway." For the first time he saw a hint of the old teasing Lacy.

"You made all this up, didn't you?" he said.

"Not all of it. Only the part about the committee."

"And the architect?" Surely, she wouldn't go so far as to make him up.

She took a sudden interest in a thread unraveling from the hem of her shirt. "I'm sure he was renowned by some. His wife, perhaps. And by me. And by you, I suspect, if you ever felt beholden to the architect who designed Hobarth Manor. The rest is true enough, or once was, at any rate, and will be again once we've saved it."

Apparently, Lacy had invented the architect. Was this just a game to her? If so, she was playing with their lives. Was she really unstable? He was torn between anger and pity.

They sat in silence for a while. "Do you remember, Pea," she said finally, "how we took turns saving each other from drowning, from sharks circling our lifeboat, or from death by starvation or sunstroke? We had a dozen scenarios we acted out on this rock."

He fixed his gaze on the dry grass tipped with frost. How had he let so much slip from his grasp? If this rock could speak, would it pity him or laugh out loud?

"We were heroes, you and I." Her voice dropped so he had to strain to hear. "Surely we can save Hobarth Manor."

"A committee of one?" he said bitterly.

"Two. You and me. Of course, Bertie can't find out, which makes me a kind of silent partner."

He sighed. "Make that a committee of three."

She looked up, questioning.

"Carlotta. One of my la…uh…one of my tenants. She brought me this. She put one in every mailbox in the neighborhood."

Lacy laughed and clapped her hands. "You see? It's working."

"But this meeting. What if people actually come? You know, the neighbors. Somebody has to take charge, and you can't even be there."

"How about…what's her name…Carlotta? Could she do it?"

Pea tried to imagine Carlotta staying on purpose long enough to conduct a meeting. Or any of his ladies, for that matter, except for Nan, and she would never do it. Nor would Fiona, who didn't like to call attention to herself.

"I suppose the logical person to lead the meeting would be you, Pea."

He shook his head. "I don't know, Lacy. I wouldn't know what to say." This was not how he was used to fixing things, through deception and swaying public opinion, exciting the emotions of others. He didn't trust it. What he trusted was the smoothness of a paint job, the quiet turn of an oiled hinge, the polish on a railing, the gleam of a clean window. Keeping things as they should be, in order, as smooth as this rock beneath his hand. He knew nothing of committees and half-truths and government agencies.

"I'll help you," Lacy said. "It will be as if I'm sitting on your shoulder directing things."

Surely this was just another game to her, Lacy up to her old tricks. He should be angry with her, but she looked so frail. He would have to talk this over with Nan. Meanwhile, there was one more thing he had to know. "The message in the ad? It said I was to save you in return."

"Yes, I did say that, didn't I?" She twisted her shirttail in her fingers, something she used to do when she was nervous. Following his glance, she smoothed the fabric over her thighs and gave it a pat. "That's for later," she said briskly. "First things first."

"No. Tell me now how I can save you." He wasn't sure he wanted to hear the answer. Didn't he have enough ladies to save?

Her shoulders slumped and her fingers began to work the fabric again.

"Is it your husband?" It wasn't like him to be so persistent, but he had to know what she expected of him.

Her laugh was without humor, dry and brittle. "You've never met Bertram Fox, have you? No, of course not. Bertie doesn't know anyone east of Wyndham Heights and I'm not supposed to, either. My mother was so happy when we became engaged. She was always afraid I'd 'go slumming,' as she put it, and not come home."

"You mean your visits here with your grandfather?"

She nodded. "I think she was actually happy he died when I was so young, before I could go off and do things by myself, because he took me everywhere. Father wouldn't let her interfere. When Grandfather died, she made him move us to Wyndham Heights."

"And I never saw you again," Pea said.

She looked up, her eyes bright with tears.

"You could have come back when you got older," he said, regretting the accusation in his tone.

"I know." Her voice was barely audible. "I could have. But by then I'd all but forgotten Hobarth Manor and you. And our rock. But I'm here now, Pea."

Pea fidgeted, wishing he were some place else. After all, she was married, and he didn't know how he felt about her anymore.

"You see," she went on, when the silence had grown heavy, "Mother won, at least for awhile. I was as impressed as she by Bertram Fox III and his family. I didn't know that polish was a veneer covering something as hard and unforgiving and determined to have its way as that wrecking ball he has planned for Hobarth Manor."

Pea looked deep into her eyes and saw what her life had been like. Even with his lack of experience and understanding about what went on between a man and his wife, he could see she had been in turn neglected and laid to waste. He saw also in the sudden set of her shoulders and the lift of her chin that maybe she could be saved. He had no idea how, but he supposed one more lady, more or less, to worry about would make little difference.

Chapter Nine

The discovery of the flyer and the signs called for another emergency meeting. It was Maizie's turn to host, and no one looked forward to that. For one thing, in spite of Nan's standing offer to send down cookies, Maizie insisted on making her own. Burned on the bottom and peppered inside with tiny bits of walnut shell, they were as hard and devoid of sweetness as Maizie herself.

Maizie kept her heavy green drapes closed, and since she was on the first floor, there were no skylights. While her apartment was clean enough, the braided rug that covered most of the hardwood floor in the living room was coming apart at the seams. And there was a prevalent odor of pine-scented air freshener, with something fishy riding underneath.

Although most of the apartment was painted a muddy beige, one wall of the living room was papered with a restless tangle of green vegetation inhabited by various jungle creatures, including an alligator benignly asleep in the lower right-hand corner. It was an uneasy reminder of the padlocked bathroom door, and the occasional splashing sound from within.

Maizie held court from an overstuffed armchair covered with a worn patchwork quilt. She had tacked up one of the flyers on the wall behind her chair, a wall filled with pinpricks from past meetings, as Maizie had a fondness for visual aids. Below the flyer a 'Save Hobarth Manor' lawn sign rested, a bit of dried mud still clinging to its wooden stake.

When they were all seated, except of course for Nan, whose name card rested on the empty chair between Pea and Sulie, Maizie cleared her throat loudly and followed up with "Come to order, please." She indicated the wall behind her. "Observe Exhibit A. For those of you who rarely go out," she said, with a pointed glance at Sulie. "Our neighborhood has been peppered with these 'Save Hobarth Manor' signs. When I saw the first one, I assumed it was a prank and I pulled it up. Then I discovered there were too many signs for one crippled old lady to remove. But it's my opinion that someone is up to no good!"

Sulie took the kitchen timer from her pocket and placed it deliberately on the coffee table, alongside the chipped milk-glass plate piled high with cookies.

"But then," Maizie continued, glaring at Sulie while the timer ticked away, "something else came to my attention. Note if you will, Exhibit B. She pointed dramatically to the flyer. Now, as I see it…" Before she could finish her sentence, the timer went off. She made a dive for it, but her arthritic knees and the easy chair, combined with Sulie's superior agility, defeated her.

A glaring silence ensued while the timer ran down. Then, as Sulie re-wound it, Fiona gave her short suede gloves a tug and adopted a soothing tone. "As Maizie no doubt sees it, and I imagine we're all inclined to agree with her," she added, with a gracious nod toward their host, "We should all plan to attend that meeting and see just who is on this committee and what their intentions are. Now…"

Maizie, still fuming, broke in. "I guess in my own home I can have my say."

"But we all agreed to keep to a time limit," Sulie protested.

"And you never set it to give me my full five minutes."

Things were getting out of hand. For the second meeting in a row, Pea took the timer away from an astonished Sulie. "I think we'll dispense with the timer again today," he said. He was sorry to take Sulie's job away, but then he wasn't anxious to have the timer set for himself. That would require him to speak, and they were bound to see he was hiding something. He had no intention of blowing Lacy's cover. "Go on, Maizie," he said. "Just keep it to the point, please, and remember you all agreed to stick together."

"And when don't I keep to the point?" Maizie said.

"When do you?" Sulie muttered, too low for Maizie to hear but perhaps loud enough for Sulie to feel she'd saved face.

"As I see it," Maizie said, "We need to show up at that meeting. Show a solid front. Protect our interests. Whoever is on this committee, you can bet they're up to no good. They probably want to save it to make it into a museum or something. I, for one, am not ready to be stuffed and put on display." With that, she clamped shut her thin mouth and folded her arms.

Carlotta spoke up. "I agree that we should all go together to this meeting. But isn't it possible that those behind this committee are the ones responsible for getting the Art Institute on the Maryland Historical Trust? Maybe this is good for us."

"But is our home of historical value?" Fiona said, adjusting her silk leopard print scarf. "How important is this Oscar Carthington?"

"Perhaps whoever is behind this is one of Trainer's old friends," Sulie put in. She was referring to her late husband, Trainer P. Rothcart. "After all, even the governor was a regular patron of The Snapper Stew and our turtle soup was well known in Baltimore's influential circles."

Maizie snorted. "What, save Hobarth Manor in honor of your soup?"

"I didn't say that, exactly," Sulie said, bristling.

"I think," Fiona said, folding her lace handkerchief into a small triangle, "Sulie is onto something. You might want to explore, dear, if any of those important people are still in positions of influence. Perhaps even the second generation?"

"That's it," Maizie said. "Find out where the bodies are buried."

"I beg your pardon?" Fiona said.

"Blackmail." Maizie rubbed her hands together. It's the only way to get City Hall on our side."

Chapter Ten

That night, as Pea was trying to sleep, he replayed the meeting in his head and was ashamed to admit that Maizie's suggestion of blackmail had a certain appeal. He tried to imagine himself as a sleuth. Disguised, perhaps as a plumber, lurking about Mr. Ryan's office, waiting for the chance to have a look at the files or the books. But what would he look for? And if he did find something incriminating, would he just steal it? No, he would get caught.

As the clock struck one, Pea listened to the ancient plumbing in the walls, to the shudder of the furnace as it clicked on and off, to the sound of water running. He even imagined he heard splashing sounds coming from Maizie's second bathroom, which was as ridiculous as the idea that Leonardo really was an alligator. But what if he was? Only Winston, the young man who came to clean Leonardo's bathtub had seen him. Once, Pea had waylaid him on the stairs and asked him, and the young man had said with a grin: "Oh, he's an alligator, all right. And a dandy, too." Could he have been serious? Pea knew better, of course, but now he found himself wondering how long alligators lived and how big a baby alligator small enough to fit in a small valise could grow in thirty years. How much danger would such a pet pose to Maizie? Of course,

Leonardo couldn't be an alligator, but what if he was something just as noxious? Soon the time was coming when he would have to invade his tenant's privacy and find out.

To calm his nerves, Pea got up and ate a whole plate of Nan's oatmeal cookies, which only set him to thinking about Nan. Just how big was she? Too big to fit through her door? Was that why she stopped going out? No, that was ridiculous. Still, she could get that big. He tried to recall the exact measurements of a standard door opening. He retrieved his yardstick from the back of the broom closet and measured the opening of his own front door. Thirty inches. He held the yardstick up to what he guessed was his widest part. Fifteen inches. But sideways he was only ten inches. Even if Nan were twice his width, she'd be able to squeeze through by moving sideways. Unless…He glanced down at his own slightly concave chest and realized how fruitless were his calculations. There was only one way to put his mind to rest. He put on his coveralls over his pajamas and tiptoed upstairs. Outside Nan's apartment, he aimed a flashlight on the doorframe. It was as he feared. In order to widen Nan's door, he'd have to cut too far into a weight-bearing wall. If it ever became necessary to use his carpenter skills to free Nan, he'd only be starting the job for the wrecking ball. He retreated in despair.

Back in bed, he listened to the wind driving tree branches against the building. He'd have to prune the ash tree to keep it from knocking against Nan's skylight. She'd never complain, of course, but it might be keeping her awake right now. The skylight. That was it. If need be, he could simply remove the skylight, enlarge the opening, and Nan could step out onto the roof. He got up there at least once a year to clear the rain gutters. But could Nan negotiate the roof? And how would he get her down? Would his ladder hold her weight? The fire department, of course. They could do it. But no, if she wouldn't have the other ladies in her apartment, she'd never consent to such a spectacle. Pea fell back onto the pillow.

What about a helicopter? Helicopters rescued injured people from mountaintops and airlifted them to the hospital. He imagined Nan being airlifted in a kind of harness. But the sidewalk below would surely be crowded with curious neighbors, some with cameras, reporters even.

But what if Nan got sick? What if there was a fire? Pea spent the rest of the night staring at the ceiling, imagining he smelled smoke, and listening for the phone to ring with the news that Nan was having chest pains. When he did sleep, he dreamed of himself and Lacy on their rock, surrounded by alligator-infested waters, while in the distance he heard Nan saying, "I just know you'll think of something, Pea."

When he dragged himself out of bed in the morning, Pea knew he was faced with a terrible task, one no man, he was sure, even one with a depth of experience with women, would ever undertake willingly. He would have to insist that Nan go on a diet.

Chapter Eleven

All thoughts of Nan were driven from Pea's head when he picked up the morning paper. The *Life and Times* section of *The Baltimore Sun* carried the headline, *Local Residents Mount Campaign to Save Neighborhood Treasure*, with a notice of the upcoming planning meeting to be held at the Art Institute. Pea scowled into his coffee. Apparently Lacy hadn't wasted any time in getting the word out. But how? She wouldn't dare give the newspaper her name. And who would conduct this meeting? Lacy was the only one capable and she couldn't do it. Not that it mattered. Who, besides his ladies, would be interested in such a meeting? Might as well leave it in the hands of Maizie for all the good it would do.

Underneath the headline was a picture of Hobarth Manor, from the days when it sported a green-and-white striped awning. A uniformed doorman helped a woman with a big feathered hat out of a chauffeur-driven 1930s Cadillac. Alongside was a second photograph, looking much the same except for the missing awning, doorman, and elegantly dressed woman. Instead there was Pea, sweeping slush from the front step. That was two days ago. Had some reporter been snooping about and taken his picture? Pea instinctively looked over his shoulder but saw only the geranium in the high basement window, a descendant of one his mother had always kept there, blooming in the morning sun.

The article noted that the nearby Rosemont Art Institute was recently listed on the Maryland Historic Trust, and wondered if Hobarth Manor was also worth saving. However, that may be a moot point, it said, as plans to demolish the apartment building to build enough condominiums to accommodate three times as many occupants was now before the zoning commission. The proposal was expected to pass with little opposition. It also mentioned Lacy's architect, and described the foyer with its black and white checkerboard marble floor. It failed to mention, of course, that as children Pea and Lacy had played checkers on that floor, using counters fashioned from pieces of felt, in an improvised game that incorporated the rules of both checkers and hopscotch.

But the memories of two children playing on a floor marbled with prismed winter light from beveled glass would do nothing to save the floor or the glass, so beautifully described by the reporter; not to mention the chandelier so exquisitely preserved and the brass inlay on what the reporter described as the formidable front door.

Formidable? His door? That was an odd way to describe it. It evidently hadn't discouraged this reporter, who speculated that the man sweeping the front step was responsible for not only the shiny brass but the overall good condition of the building as a whole. At that, the article ran out of steam.

To Pea's relief, the reporter evidently hadn't gotten any further than the foyer viewed through the front door. However, in small print beneath the text was the promise that this was only the first in a series of pieces. The next was to focus on the group of elderly people who still occupied Hobarth Manor, senior citizens who would be set adrift in their declining years if the owner had his way. A side issue, the paper suggested, of some human interest.

So, the reporter planned to stalk his ladies. As alarming as that idea was to Pea, even more disturbing was the idea that the building itself constituted the great emergency. Evidently the public should decide if the bricks and mortar of Hobarth Manor should outlast the needs of some old people who wouldn't be here that long. The article didn't say that, not exactly, but wasn't it missing the point? The flyers should read, "Save Nan, Save Maizie, Save Fiona, Save Sulie, Save Pea." They were flesh and blood, with feelings and memories of hopscotch in the foyer, the feel of ivory keys beneath spread fingers, the smell of Nan's homemade bread in the hall, and the taste of her lemon meringue pie for Sunday morning breakfast.

Paper in hand, Pea sat and thought about this stunning revelation as a cold truth seeped in from the stone floor beneath the thin wool carpet. It crept into his toes and worked its way up to his heart. For the truth was, the bricks and mortar was the thing. Their perceived importance by a public distracted by its own memories was the only means of saving his ladies.

Pea put down the paper and looked at the phone. Soon it would ring. Or Maizie would lean on his doorbell and yell from the top of the steps that the contents of the morning paper necessitated another meeting of the Hobarth Tenant's Association. No, this time he wouldn't wait for someone else to shove him into action. He dialed Lacy's number, hoping she would pick up the phone. He didn't want to be one of those men who hangs up if the husband answers.

Lacy did answer. "Look, this is more complicated than you can guess," Pea said. "All this publicity. I have to protect my..." He stopped, lest he pick up the newspaper and read that the caretaker refers to the elderly tenants as "his ladies." Never mind that Pea had only used the term in his own mind; he felt the invasion of the article so keenly that he wouldn't be surprised to find the very contents of his mind spilled across the front page of the *Life and Times* section. "To protect my tenants," he finished.

"From what?" Lacy said. "I thought you wanted to protect them from homelessness."

"But that reporter means to write about them. I know you put her up to it. What did you tell her?"

He could almost see Lacy throw up her small hands. "You know I have to remain anonymous," she said. "Did you see my name anywhere?"

"Lacy?"

She giggled. "As I understand it, a concerned citizen called in the information."

"And what, exactly, did this 'concerned citizen' tell the reporter?"

"Only that Carlotta was a noted concert pianist in her day, a graduate from the Art Institute down the street, and that the others may also be of interest."

"Nothing else?" He almost asked Lacy if she'd told the reporter about Nan's refusing to leave her apartment, but decided it was better not to give her ideas about Nan.

"Of course not, Pea." Lacy's voice was all innocence. He was reminded of the old days, when her pretty eyes would widen, her eyebrows would go up, and her mouth form an amazed little "0" whenever she was confronted with an obvious deception. It was only later that Pea realized he hadn't told Lacy about Carlotta, either.

After he hung up, Pea calmed himself by carrying carton after carton to the curb for the Salvation Army. Suddenly obsessed with unburdening himself of unnecessary baggage, he was beginning to be almost eager to move on.

Chapter Twelve

Pea usually had little patience for the tenant meetings, but this time he called one himself, grateful, at least, that it was Fiona's turn to play hostess. Eccentric though she may be; of all the ladies, he found her the easiest to deal with. Except for Nan, or course, who just now was no help at all. He put on clean socks with no holes, as Fiona required them to leave their shoes in her entry in order to protect her white carpet.

Fiona's French Provincial dining-room chairs were arranged in a semi-circle around her glass-topped coffee table. Pea took his assigned seat, next to Nan's vacant chair. Maizie, wearing scratchy-looking wool socks with a moth hole in one heel, was on the end, well away from Sulie, on Pea's left. Carlotta, in pink crocheted slippers, sat on the other side of Nan's empty chair.

Fiona, dressed in yellow lounging pajamas with matching ballet slippers, arranged a tray of Nan's cookies and brownies on the coffee table. She was about to take a seat and open the meeting when the doorbell rang.

"Were you expecting someone?" Sulie asked. "It's not that reporter, is it?"

"If it is, get rid of him," Maizie grumbled. "We don't want him at our meeting."

Somehow Pea knew who it was, even before he heard Lacy's voice from the hall. "Fiona, I can hardly believe it's really you. I'm so pleased you're still here." She sailed into the living room, Fiona trailing behind, her face a study in confusion.

"Why, my dear, I don't see where we could have possibly met," Fiona was saying.

How Lacy found out about the meeting, Pea didn't know, but it obviously wasn't Fiona. He suspected Carlotta, who refused to meet his gaze. Obviously Maizie hadn't invited her, not from the way she sat with her heavy arms crossed and her wool socks planted firmly on the floor. She glared at Lacy.

"I don't know that we actually ever met," Lacy said, "but I used to visit here...my goodness, that was so long ago...you looked like a movie star...I loved to see you all dressed up. And you always were. And your friend used to give me candy. Why, come to think of it, that was you in that old photograph in this morning's newspaper, wasn't it?" Lacy said. That was your friend's car."

Pea remembered how Lacy had always stopped whatever game they were playing to stare at Fiona as she came down the stairs, her elegantly dressed feet placed just so on the steps, her long neck supporting an amazing hat over her classic features. When she returned, Lacy would watch the chauffer help her from the shiny black car. Pea had forgotten how the older man who sometimes accompanied her up the walk would offer them each a handful of pink peppermints. Of course, Lacy would have recognized Fiona and the car immediately when she saw the paper. Why she pretended surprise just now, Pea couldn't imagine, except the Lacy he knew as a child would often offer a lie when the truth would have been more believable.

Maizie scowled. "What's going on, here? Are we going to have a meeting, or what? Who is this person?"

Before an obviously flustered Fiona could answer, Pea took control of the situation, a control he sensed would not last. "Fiona,

55

I'd like you to meet Lacy Myers, I mean, Fox. Mrs. Bertram Fox. She used to visit with her grandfather, Mr. Myers."

"That's right," Lacy said with a smile in his direction. "Pea and I were children together. And I'm on the Committee to Preserve Hobarth Manor. Fiona, I'm so pleased to see you. I just assumed that all the former tenants would have moved away long ago."

"As indeed some have, my dear," Fiona said. She may have recovered her dignity, but she clearly didn't share Lacy's delight in the reunion. "Allow me to introduce Maizie, Carlotta, and Sulie," she said stiffly, pointing them out in turn.

"What a lovely apartment. Is that the original embossed wallpaper?" said Lacy. "That's a Toulouse Lautrec, isn't it?" She indicated a print on the wall, a stylized image of a woman with long trailing gloves.

Fiona nodded as she discreetly removed Nan's nametag and motioned Lacy to the empty chair next to Pea. She managed a thin smile. "As long as you're here," she said politely, "perhaps you'd like to take a seat."

Maizie bit off a question. "So. You're the granddaughter. That makes you the heir, right? So, what are you doing here? Measuring the place to see how many cars you can park in Fiona's living room once you've paved us all over?"

For a moment, Lacy looked as if she were about to run out the door. Then, straightening her back, she said evenly, "I know it looks bad, Maizie, but you must understand, I have no control over the property. I'd do anything to help you keep your home."

"What do you mean, you have no control?" Maizie said. The others nodded as if the same question had just occurred to them.

"It's complicated," Pea said quickly. "Take her word for it; right now, there's nothing she can do." Why did he feel he had to protect her when she lied about the least little thing? Still, he felt a tender warmth at her grateful glance.

"I think perhaps we had best get on with the meeting," Fiona said. "And the first thing on the agenda should be how we can avoid any further intrusion into our lives by that reporter."

"But isn't the publicity good for us?" Carlotta asked.

Lacy looked up from studying the minutes of the last meeting, handed to her by the gracious Fiona. "Publicity is essential. But, of course, one's privacy must be respected," she added, with a nod toward Fiona, who looked doubtful. "But Maizie, I see here that you suggested the possibility of blackmail. Excellent idea."

Maizie leaned forward, forgetting, for the moment, her antagonism toward this intruder. "What about the old geezers on the zoning commission? I'll bet my knee-high stockings there's plenty of dirt there for somebody with enough stomach to do the digging."

"I'll take charge of that," Lacy said smoothly, "and I'll let you know if I come up with something."

Muttering to herself, Maizie pressed her lips together.

Smiling serenely and turning from Maizie, Lacy addressed the others. "Perhaps we could organize some kind of protest to get the public's attention."

"Humph," said Maizie.

"That hardly seems dignified," sniffed Fiona.

"I rarely go out," Sulie put in.

"And I have Leonardo to look after," Maizie said. At Lacy's questioning look, she added casually, with a sidelong glance as if to gauge the level of fear this engendered in the room. "My pet alligator."

"Oh wonderful!" Carlotta said. "I suppose you're going to tell that reporter you're harboring an illegal pet."

"No such thing," Maizie protested, "although I believe there's almost as much human interest in my Leonardo, who has spent the last thirty years in a bathtub and who has been a worthy companion for a lonely widow deserted by her ungrateful daughter, as there is interest in a has-been concert pianist."

"Most assuredly, Maizie," Lacy said soothingly, "but unless we can figure out a way to feed the reporter to Leonardo, perhaps we'd best keep him under wraps for the time being." The nervous laughter that followed Lacy's suggestion defused some of the tension. Even Maizie loosened her grip on her elbows.

What I have in mind," Lacy said, "is a nice peaceful—that is," she added, with a nod toward Fiona, "dignified march. Somewhere where there's a lot of pedestrian traffic. Perhaps a mall. Now, do any of you have a walker or a cane you could use? It would help build sympathy for your cause."

While the ladies stared at Lacy as if she had just asked them to grow tails, Pea tried to reconcile this delicate whirlwind, alert and observant, with the shrinking, faded creature he had run into just days ago. Was she on some new medication? Was this behavior a symptom of some mental state and the other woman the real Lacy, or was it the other way around? And why would a bunch of elderly people marching around help their cause? At any rate, it was time for a change of subject, which reminded him of why he'd called the meeting. He held up the flyer advertising the planning meeting. "What about this? Somebody has to take charge."

"Why, that would be you, Pea," Lacy said airily.

Pea opened his mouth to object, but realized he was fixed in the gaze of four of his ladies, who depended upon him, it seemed, for their very survival. He swallowed.

"Don't worry, Pea," Lacy said, "I'll write a nice little opening speech for you. It'll be easy."

Easy for her to say. Just thinking about it, he felt perspiration gathering in his armpits.

"Perhaps it's time for me to help you pick out that new suit, Pea," Fiona said gently.

He slumped in his chair. Clearly, there was no escaping his responsibility, which every day seemed to require abilities beyond him.

Just then, Lacy noticed the name card Fiona had placed on the table and picked it up. "But where is Nan?" she said.

"Nan never comes to our meetings," Fiona said, passing a tray of brownies. "She sends food, but the only one she sees these days is Pea."

"Really? Why is that, Pea?"

Before he could think of a suitable lie, Carlotta came to the rescue. "Nan studied under Lawrence Arlington," she said. "At the Institute. That was well before my time, of course. I understand she had a couple of shows before moving back home to care for her father. The fate, I'm afraid, of so many talented women." She put down the brownie she was about to bite into, as if that sad thought had taken away her appetite.

"But she kept on with her painting?" Lacy said.

"Up until a few years ago," Pea said.

"For her own enjoyment, only," Carlotta sighed. "Like my music. I'm afraid Nan and I both missed out on the full blossoming of our careers."

"So," Lacy mused, "Hobarth Manor is the home of a famous pianist and a painter. Fiona, of course, has style. And Sulie, what is your special talent?"

Sulie looked embarrassed. "I'm afraid I'm not at all artistic," she said. Her carelessly chopped-off white hair and mismatched clothing testified to that.

"Sulie was once the proprietor of a famous restaurant," Fiona said. "Perhaps you've heard of *The Snapper Stew*? Famous for its turtle soup?"

Lacy looked blank for a moment, then recovered. "Why yes, I have. My grandfather loved that place. I don't think I've had turtle soup since I was eight-years-old." She looked around the room.

Pea sighed. A likely fib, totally unnecessary.

"Maybe we should consider how to put all your talents to work," Lacy said.

Maizie bristled. "And just where do I fit into these grand plans? I didn't realize I was living among such important people. Perhaps Leonardo and I should just move out." She had uncrossed her arms, but sat with her blunt fingers spread on her knees, ready to do battle.

Pea could almost hear the other ladies thinking, "Oh, if only she would," as they gazed at the napkins in their laps or rolled crumbs beneath their fingers.

"Why Maizie," Lacy said smoothly. "I was just going to suggest a job for you. We're going to need someone with people skills to organize that picket brigade. Do you think you can do that?"

They all looked at Lacy in astonishment, everyone except for Maizie, who came very close to actually beaming her pleasure at being at last recognized for her people skills. Sulie opened her mouth to object, but Pea silenced her with a shake of his head. Perhaps Maizie had met her match. As for the upcoming meeting at the Art Institute, he'd go with Fiona to buy the suit, but they'd just have to find someone else to take charge.

Chapter Thirteen

Lacy's prepared speech in hand, Pea stood before his mother's full-length mirror and cleared his throat. "Good afternoon, ladies and gentlemen," he said. "Thank you for giving up your Sunday afternoon for the worthy cause of saving Hobarth Manor. That noble establishment has graced our neighborhood for over half a century. The work of the esteemed architect Oscar Carthington, it represents an era when attention to design and artistry, not to mention pride of workmanship and quality of materials, was paramount. Those days, my friends, are long gone, and now the question we have to ask ourselves is this: Are we going to allow this neighborhood treasure to go down with the wrecking ball?"

Pea stopped. Something was wrong. Perhaps it was his grey work shirt and his cowlick. He put down the notes and combed his hair. Then he got into his new pale blue suit with a white shirt and red-and-blue-striped tie. He'd had in mind something more conservative, perhaps a navy pinstripe, but Fiona had insisted on this blue. To set off his eyes, she'd said.

Yes, that was better. "You're quite the handsome fool, Percival Jamieson McNulty," he said aloud to the mirror. "All dressed up to go on a fool's errand." He wouldn't be doing this if Lacy hadn't come back into his life, and he wondered, not for the first time, if this wasn't just another of their childhood games. At least now he was dressed for the part. He took up the speech. "Good afternoon," he began, intrigued by how the new suit added resonance to his voice. Still, the words were not his. If only Lacy dared go to the meeting.

His doorbell rang and he heard Maizie call out, "Pea, we're ready. Are you coming?"

He stuffed the notes into his pocket, patted down his hair, and put on the grey fedora Fiona had insisted went with his new look.

"Pea, for god's sake, are you in there?" Maizie called. He's taking a nap. I knew it. He fell asleep and didn't wake up to get ready."

"Coming. Just now coming," he shouted back. One of these days he was going to have a little talk with Maizie about her thinking he was at her beck and call. As he emerged from his apartment, he caught four looks of approval.

They made a parade, he noted with some embarrassment, as they walked to the Art Institute for the imaginary meeting of the imaginary committee to save what would soon exist only in the imaginations or memories of those who cared, and precious few there were, and none with any power. But he had to admit he felt, in his new suit and hat, if not powerful, then at least visible. Fiona, wearing a fitted grey wool coat trimmed in mink and black leather gloves with matching boots, linked her arm through his.

Fiona had wanted to outfit the others, but Lacy had said no, they'd get more sympathy as they were dressed, so there was Maizie in her frayed wool plaid jacket with a dingy headscarf, with a walker provided by Lacy. Occasionally forgetting she was supposed to be pushing it, she would pick it up and carry it until Carlotta or Fiona, who marched on either side of her, nudged a reminder. Carlotta was in a moth-eaten fur coat that bounced against her ankles. Sulie wore her late husband's trench coat, rolled up at the sleeves.

At the Institute they followed signs to the meeting room Lacy had rented, where Pea was surprised to see a couple dozen people. They mingled about a table spread with Nan's cakes and cookies. They were mostly elderly, a good many with canes or walkers. At one end of the table there was a jar labeled 'Donations'.

A smug-looking Maizie, who obviously enjoyed Pea's surprise at the turn-out, explained. "They're from the senior center where I go to play bingo. I told them there'd be treats. All they get is packaged cookies and some of them are on special diets and never get anything good."

"Well done, Maizie," he said, although he couldn't imagine how these people were to be of help to them. He was about to suggest they all have a piece of cake and call it a day when another dozen or so drifted in. He wondered how Lacy had managed to round them up. Then a young man approached him.

"You must be Mr. McNulty," he said. "I represent The *Baltimore Sun*. I'll be covering your meeting. Do you mind?" Before Pea could figure out what he wasn't supposed to mind, the reporter had produced a camera and snapped his picture. With the reporter there, Pea had no choice but to take his place in front of the gathering, a signal for the guests to be seated with their snack-filled plates.

"Well, let's see, uh," Pea said, rummaging in his pocket for his speech. He smoothed it out on the lectern and cleared his throat. "Ladies and Gentlemen," he began. He cleared his throat once more. "Thank you for giving up your Sunday afternoon for the, uh, the worthy, uh…" His face grew warm at the prospect of reading what came next. Who would believe such eloquence coming from him? No one, certainly not the bored looking reporter. But he had to say something, if only for the sake of the new suit. So, he put aside Lacy's notes and dove in. "Uh, I'm Pea; that is, Percival McNulty, and I've lived all my life at Hobarth Manor and for most of my life—well, after the war, anyway—I've tried to take good care of it; and these ladies here have been there, too, for a long time. Now Hobarth Manor is not just our home. It's, well, it's..." and now he felt at a loss, for he hadn't ever thought about exactly what it was. But, noticing the reporter had taken out his notepad, he took heart and went on. "Hobarth Manor is, well, it's different. There's lots of nice things about it. Statues, for one thing. Ladies holding everything up, or at least that's the way it's always seemed to me. And lots of windows I keep clean and which my father also kept clean. And real good wood all over, with a grain you don't see much of anymore."

The audience was listening and nodding and the reporter was scribbling. Warming to his subject, Pea spoke faster. "And carvings all over the place. Acorns and pineapples and such. And fancy wallpaper and, well, I guess it was built by this architect." He consulted Lacy's speech. "Oscar Carthington, his name was." Out of words, he scanned the rest of the text and found one useful word: treasure. "Some might say Hobarth Manor is a treasure. But I say it's home and I hope you will help us save it." With that, he sat down, knowing he should have tied things up and wishing Lacy were here to do it.

He needn't have worried, for Maizie was making her way to the front, not only remembering to push the walker, but dragging her left leg a bit. Was she overdoing it?

When she reached the microphone, Maizie fixed the gathering with her little black eyes and said, "Now, here's what we do. I want you all to meet me at the mall at 10:00 sharp on Wednesday. Bring your walkers and your wheelchairs and your friends. I'll supply the signs." She raised her fist and shouted into the reporter's raised camera, "Save Hobarth manor!"

There was a brief pause while Maizie scowled at the ladies in the front row. Finally, Fiona managed a weak, "Save Hobarth Manor," followed by a hesitant Carlotta, then Sulie, who nudged Pea in the side. To his relief, the audience took up the cry, saving him from the embarrassment of joining in. Then, an old man in back of the room, who looked to be in his nineties, struggled to his feet and yelled out, "To the barricades!"

Soon the room, powered by Nan's sugar and the seniors' own long lost struggles, was filled with the sound of revolution. Pea made for the back door, his bewildered ladies following. Except for Maizie, who stayed to talk to the reporter and work the crowd. Pea could only hope she would avoid the subject of Leonardo.

Chapter Fourteen

It was bedtime at Hobarth Manor, but the meeting at the Art Institute had left everyone wound up and reluctant to take leave of one another. They were gathered in Sulie's kitchen, which took up most of her apartment space, the wall between it and the living room having been removed twenty years ago, when Sulie moved in. The round table, with its dozen Shaker style chairs, was spread with goodies rescued from the hungry revolutionaries.

The walls of Sulie's kitchen were decorated with framed restaurant reviews of The Snapper Stew and pictures of Sulie's husband, the late Trever P. Rothcart, wearing his chef's hat and smiling alongside well-fed dignitaries. One clipping showed a young, almost unrecognizable Sulie, standing next to a menu board. And resting on a pedestal table near the door was a curious memento: an oaken stick about three inches in diameter and a foot long, with what appeared to be teeth marks around its middle.

Floor-to-ceiling cookbooks took up one wall, although it had been years since Sulie had used them for anything other than reading matter. More cookbooks were spread out over the floor next to a rocking chair facing a small television. Heavy restaurant-style dishes were stacked on open shelves, alongside rows of Campbell's soup and a large economy-sized box of Saltines. The kitchen boasted two sinks, two refrigerators, and copper-bottomed pans of all sizes hung from cast iron frames; but except for a single saucepan on the stove, there was little evidence much actual cooking took place. The otherwise spotless countertop held only an electric can opener.

"Would anyone like some soup?" Sulie asked, and seeing there were no takers, she set out some cheese and a plate of crackers alongside the leftover sweets.

"I'm sorry I didn't give your speech," Pea told Lacy, who had been waiting for them back at the Manor.

"I know," she said. "I was hiding in a closet off the meeting room. I heard everything and I think you were fine. And the suit, well, it suits you."

Pea felt his face grow warm and was grateful Maizie chose that moment to dump the jar of donations onto the table, spilling a few coins on the floor. By the time he'd chased them down, he'd regained his composure.

"It's hardly enough to bribe the zoning commission," Maizie said. "But it's a start."

"A start toward what?" Fiona asked.

"A start toward saving this place, of course," Maizie said. "We need money for that, don't we?"

"Yes, but how exactly would we use the money, supposing we got some?"

"Fiona's right," Lacy said. "We need a plan of action."

"How about getting Hobarth Manor listed as a valuable historical site?" Carlotta said. "Like the Art Institute. Would that require an attorney? Lawyers cost money."

"I did a little research on that," Lacy said. She took a notepad from her shirt pocket. "In my opinion, Hobarth Manor does meet some of these criteria: 'Integrity of design, workmanship, and artistic value.' And, it is well over fifty years old."

"So how do we get it listed?" Fiona asked.

Lacy spoke haltingly, with her eyes downcast. "That's a little complicated. Ordinarily, as the owner, I could recommend its nomination to the State Review Board."

"Well then?" Maize said.

"It just so happens, you see, at the moment, I don't have control over the property. Unless my father's trustee agrees, the Review Board would decline to consider it."

Pea could see how it pained her to not only admit her own helplessness, but that it was her husband who wanted to destroy their home.

Maizie's eyes narrowed. "What kind of a deal is that?" She turned to Pea. "Is she any use to us at all?"

Pea couldn't honestly say if she was, but the tears standing in her eyes had to be dealt with. He drew up tall in his chair, aware of the authority bestowed by the new suit, and fixed Maizie with the sternest look he could muster. "Lacy is responsible for today's meeting at the Art Institute and the reporter. And she's here. She cares what happens to Hobarth Manor, and she cares what happens to you. Now, if anyone has anything else to say, get on with it." He glanced at the clock on the wall. It had been a very long day and he dearly wanted it to end, but he didn't dare leave them to their own devices.

Sulie raised a tentative hand. "If it's money we need, perhaps Carlotta could give a benefit concert."

"Oh, but my dear," Carlotta said, absently poking one long finger in a smattering of cracker crumbs, "It's been years since I played in public. I couldn't possibly…"

Maizie smirked at Sulie. "Any more hare-brained ideas?"

Sulie drew herself up and Pea got ready to disrupt the oncoming battle, but Lacy distracted Sulie with a gentle pat. "It's an excellent idea, Sulie, but if Carlotta doesn't feel…"

"Of course, I could play some Beethoven, with perhaps a little Bach," Carlotta put in quickly.

"Wonderful," Lacy said. "Perhaps we could hold it at the Art Institute. I have a friend on the Board of Directors." She frowned and tapped her forehead with her pen, a mannerism familiar to Pea from their homework sessions and a sign she was lost in thought. Not necessarily a good sign, but at least the tears were gone. Brightening, she began to scribble. "Art Institute Celebrates Famous Graduate in a Benefit Concert for the Save the Hobarth Manor Project."

By now, Carlotta was beaming. "I'll finish up with Mozart."

"How about 'Three Blind Mice?" Maizie said. "Better pick at least one thing you can play."

"Oh, and what will you do?" Carlotta challenged her.

"Maizie can be a kind of roving special assistant," Lacy put in quickly.

Maizie, apparently forgetting for the moment her antagonism toward a potentially useless Lacy, threw Carlotta a triumphant look.

"I've got another idea," Lacy said. "We could serve food. I'm not talking about cookies and punch made from Seven-up and sherbet, but a sit-down dinner. With a world famous restaurateur to oversee the food preparation."

"Who would that be?" Fiona said. Who do we know?"

"Why, paraphernalia Sulie, of course." Lacy gestured toward the framed reviews amid all the cooking paraphernalia. "Aren't you the former proprietor of the famous Snapper Stew in downtown Philadelphia?"

Sulie frowned. "But my dear, that was so long ago. It's been almost twenty years since my husband…" Her voice trailed off.

"Blood poisoning," Maizie supplied enthusiastically. "He met his match in a snapping turtle he meant for the stew pot."

By now Sulie was near tears. "My poor Trevor. His commitment to quality was his downfall. He insisted on only the freshest of ingredients, and one day, when he was about to cut off the head of a turtle, he held out the stick…" She waved her hand toward the stick mounted on the pedestal. "He held the stick for the turtle to grasp, to keep its teeth away from his hands. He miscalculated, and before he knew it, the turtle had two of his fingers."

Fiona sighed and Carlotta rolled her eyes. This wasn't the first time they'd heard the story or Trevor's demise.

Lacy handed Sulie a tissue. "You were famous," she said gently, "for your turtle soup. Also, I understand, your key lime pie. Wouldn't it be wonderful if we could revive the tradition?"

Sulie dried her eyes and shook her head sadly. "I don't know where I'd find a live snapping turtle."

"Perhaps frozen?"

"Oh no. Only the freshest of ingredients will do. Only if I could kill the creature myself." Her eyes glazed over as she pantomimed the neat slice to the turtle's neck, followed by a flick of her wrist. "Out of the question," she muttered. "Out of the question."

Pea couldn't agree more. He couldn't picture Sulie doing any food preparation that didn't involve a can opener, even if they did find the money to put on such an event.

"Never mind," Lacy said. "We'll work out the menu. The important thing is, we'll have your expertise. And your reputation to draw on for publicity. And Fiona, since this is all about preserving what is beautiful and worthwhile from the past, perhaps you can be in charge of the decorations and the table settings."

Pleased, Fiona nodded. "Perhaps I could arrange a vintage fashion show."

"Oh yes, you should see her closet," Carlotta said. "But what about Nan? She was well known locally in her day. We could show her paintings."

"Wait a minute," Pea said. "You know how Nan values her privacy."

"That's right," Maizie said. "If she won't even show herself in public, what makes you think she'll show her precious paintings?"

"You'll just have to persuade her, Pea," Lacy said.

"I'll talk to her," he sighed. He'd agree to almost anything that would end this meeting. He swept the table with what he hoped was a very stern look. "But nobody—I mean nobody— says a word about Nan's paintings without her permission."

"Well," Lacy said briskly, "that settles it. We'll do a benefit concert at the Institute and combine it with a banquet, the food prepared under the supervision of the former proprietor and chef of the famous Snapper Stew of Philadelphia. If Nan agrees, we'll combine it with a showing of the noted painter…"

"Natalie Fisher, former student of the renowned Lawrence Arlington Washburn," Carlotta supplied.

"Ah, yes. We'll have to advertise, of course. If any donations come in, we can use them for that. And we can sell tickets in advance." She sat back with a sigh of satisfaction.

Pea remembered how she always made up the rules for their games. Now, fifty years later, he wondered if this was not another case of her imagination running free. Perhaps, at Lacy's whim, they'd go through the motions of saving Hobarth Manor and the wrecking ball would still arrive on time without any of them figuring out where they would go. It was nearly April, and the deadline was sometime in July.

Chapter Fifteen

Pea was raking winter debris from the flowerbeds when Maizie came up the sidewalk. She carried a 'Save Hobarth Manor' placard under one arm, the walker under the other, and her cracked patent leather purse under her chin. Pea relieved her of both the placard and the walker.

"You should have been there, Pea," she chortled. "I'd give my next social security check to have it on video."

Pea put down the walker, expecting the worst. Maizie could only be this happy for some perverse reason. It was the first day for what the ladies called the picketing brigade, and all morning he'd been uneasy, thinking he should have gone to the mall to protect Maizie. Or more to the point, to protect the public from her.

"First of all," she began, "your Lacy is brilliant, just brilliant, for coming up with this picketing idea. Some of those old folks were activists in their day. There's this ninety-year-old man—sharp as a tack, although a little hard of hearing and a bit confused about the cause—he kept going on about the bonus Mr. Hoover owed him from World War I. But spry as a grasshopper and quite willing to take orders. You know, Pea, willingness to take orders, to be a good follower? That's very important for movement cohesiveness."

Obviously Maizie had been the one giving orders. Pea leaned on the walker for support. "How many, exactly, turned out?"

"About twenty in all, although no more than five joined in the picketing at any one time. I, of course, kept right on when the others took their coffee breaks and potty breaks. And a good thing too, because I don't know what they would have done when that pompous security guard showed up. Do you know, Pea, he had a gun. Do you think I could get one?"

Pea pushed the walker over to the bench and sank down. He imagined a prostrate and bleeding security guard, while Maizie somehow made a get-away in the midst of blazing sirens, leaving a confused World War I veteran to take the rap. He took a deep breath. "You'd best sit down, Maizie, and tell me what happened. What did you do?" He glanced down the street, half expecting a police car to pull up. Perhaps he should usher Maizie inside.

Maizie sat down and wedged her handbag between them. "Oh, before I forget, Pea." She pulled from her purse an envelope stuffed with dollar bills and checks and loose change and handed it over. "The day's take."

The image of the unconscious security guard now grew to include Maizie wielding his pilfered gun and holding up the proprietor of the Orange Julius concession. "Maizie, tell me about the security guard."

"I must say you don't seem very impressed. Aren't you even going to count it?"

Pea stuffed the money into his jacket. Protecting his ladies had never been so difficult. "Later, Maizie. Tell me. Now."

"Oh, all right. This little toad approached me after we'd been there about an hour and asked if we had permission to be there. I said no, but I guess we had the rights of any other American citizen, and getting old didn't specifically rob us of those rights. He kind of smirked and said, you know, talking down to me, he asked if we had a license to picket there. The old folks were trembling in their Depends. I leaned on my walker like, you know, I'd fall down without it, and by this time we had quite an audience. He looked a little nervous, so I just let the crowd gather so there'd be plenty of witnesses." She paused for breath. "Then I said, 'Young man, have you ever heard of the Pruneyard decision?'"

"The what?" Pea said, wondering what prunes had to do with anything.

"Robins vs. Pruneyard," Maizie said with authority. "First Amendment protection guaranteed by the California Supreme Court." She smirked. "Of course, I didn't tell him it was a California decision. Who knows what they have here in Maryland?"

"Maizie, where did you get all this?"

"Carlene, from the old folks home. She's an old activist from California. She said if we were challenged, we maybe could use it for a bluff. And she was right. He sort of melted away, shaking his head to think an old lady like myself with a walker would know her rights."

"And that was all?" Pea said. "You didn't do or say anything else? And the money?"

"All legit contributions, Pea. That old gasbag of a security guard did us a favor. When he left, I gave that crowd an earful, let me tell you…"

"That's okay, Maizie," he interrupted. "You've had a big day and a job well done. You deserve a rest now." In fact, she looked capable of a full day's work. He, however, was exhausted.

Chapter Sixteen

"What shall I do with this?" Pea asked Lacy, as they sat on their rock in the park.

Lacy fished a handful of bills and a few checks from the brown paper bag and quickly counted it. "Why Pea, there's almost $2,000.00 here."

After the publicity following the meeting at the Art Institute, letters began to arrive addressed, "To Whom it May Concern at Hobarth Manor." In other words, to Pea. They contained expressions of support accompanied by contributions, mostly fives and tens, with a few large bills and checks.

We'll have to open an account," Lacy said.

"Fine. You do it." He thrust the bag at her. The money made him nervous.

She pushed it away. "No, the account has to be in *your* name. We'll get a P.O. box number for future contributions." She frowned. "I should have done this before, but somehow I didn't…" Her voice trailed off in confusion.

"You didn't think anyone would take this seriously, did you?" he said.

"I don't know what I thought, honestly, Pea. I just followed an impulse. You see these signs around, you know, save this or save that and the next thing you know there's a notice in the paper that a new building has been put under the protection of the historical society. So, when I heard what Bertram had in mind for Hobarth Manor, I just went out and had those signs made. And then the flyers. And the Art Institute seemed like the logical place to display them. The people there were so nice and accommodating." She brightened. "Did I tell you, Pea, they're going to let us have the benefit there?"

"And the architect?" Pea asked, a new feeling of dread creeping up his spine. Somehow the research she claimed to have done didn't quite fit with the random actions she just described.

Lacy frowned. "What about him?"

"I never heard about Hobarth Manor being designed by a famous architect. Doesn't that seem a bit strange to you?"

Lacy shifted her weight on the rock. "You know, Pea? This stone is really cold." She gave an exaggerated shiver. "I feel it through my wool coat. We've got to find a more comfortable place to meet."

"Lacy," Pea persisted, recognizing her old tactic of distract and withdraw. But she headed him off by glancing at her watch and looking genuinely shocked. "Would you look at the time! I have to go. I'll call you. Bye." She jumped down and took off across the park, her feet sinking into the wet mattress of leaves and pine needles. A thin strip of white flesh showed between the tops of her boots and the hem of her camel-colored coat. Pea watched her go, touched, as always, by her thinness, her nervous energy, and the quick way her mind turned from one thing to another, while his plodded on. He stuffed the bag of money into the inside pocket of his overcoat and headed home, the architect momentarily forgotten.

Chapter Seventeen

Before long, the bank account showed a balance large enough to hire an attorney, who drafted a strongly worded letter to Bertram Fox, threatening court action if he proceeded to tear down Hobarth Manor before its historical value could be determined.

Meanwhile, Pea and Lacy fell into the habit of meeting at the park several times a week. Even today, after the temperature dipped twenty-six degrees, unseasonable for mid-April, and the path was ankle deep in snow from a rare late storm. Pea noticed, from his perch, their separate footprints leading to the rock, his large with deep overshoe treads, hers dainty with the impress of her high-heeled boots with narrow, pointed toes.

Lacy sat close to him, her hands captured by an old-fashioned muff Fiona had given her when she showed up one day without gloves, her hands blue from the cold.

"Bertie's beside himself," she said gleefully. "You should have seen him when he opened that letter from the attorney. He paced up and down, swearing he'd find whoever is behind the movement. He says that weasel of a caretaker—that's you, Pea—and those decrepit, senile old ladies aren't capable of mounting such an organized attack, and someone else must be the brains."

"And he doesn't suspect you at all?"

"Are you kidding? He thinks I'm too spaced out on sedatives and pain medication to add two and two. He doesn't know I haven't taken a pill for almost a month."

"No headaches?"

"Nothing I can't live with. Funny, isn't it? It just goes to show how observant Bertie is. He always did underestimate me. You know, Pea, I've been thinking maybe that's what caused my headaches. Being underestimated. Never having my opinion taken into account. Maybe if we'd had children..." her voice trailed off on a sad note, then went quickly on. "I've been a cipher, Pea, for a long time." She laughed. "And now it works in our favor, you see, because I can do whatever I like as long as I behave as if I'm in a medicated haze when he's around."

"Why are you doing this, Lacy? You're taking an awful chance."

She considered for a moment while she watched a cardinal on a snow-covered tree branch. "I think in the beginning I just wanted to make trouble. I objected to him tearing down Hobarth manor and he simply brushed my feelings aside. He said I had no head for business, then he laughed and said I had no head at all. That's when I started formulating a plan. Well, not exactly a plan. I thought I'd just put out a few flyers and signs and see what happened. Be a thorn in his side. I never thought I could actually do anything. Then I saw you and visited Hobarth Manor and spent time with those wonderful Ladies. Even Maizie. I just can't let them down. And just imagine, Pea," she turned toward him, her eyes alight, "No pills for a whole month."

"Is that what you meant by "I'll save you and you save me?"

"Maybe. Unconsciously, of course. I didn't know then..." She was crying now and Pea reached over and held his handkerchief to her face so she could blow, like a child, without taking her hands from the warmth of the muff.

Chapter Eighteen

The day the reporter came, Pea refused to answer his doorbell or the phone. He ignored Maizie when she planted herself at the top of the steps and bellowed his name, "a charming ritual," as noted in the article that appeared a few days later under the caption, "The Hobarth Manor Tenant's Association."

Evidently the ladies had gathered in Carlotta's apartment, for there was a picture of her seated at her grand piano dressed in black crepe. The reporter made much of her graduation from the Art Institute and noted that the fundraising committee, headed by the energetic and resourceful Maizie, planned to hold a concert there.

All in all, it was a harmless bit of reporting, Pea thought, as he scanned the part about Fiona's impeccable style and Sulie's culinary history. But he squirmed in discomfort at her description of Maizie fuming at the top of the steps, muttering, "He's down there, all right. Hiding from us, that's what."

The reporter ended with a promise of a future piece on the elusive Percival Jamieson McNulty, affectionately known as Peanut, or Pea. He hated to see his nickname in print, but forgot his embarrassment at the next paragraph, which mentioned Nan, "the talented recluse on the third floor, an accomplished artist who apparently hasn't left her apartment for some years, due to obesity. Rumor has it she can no longer fit through the door."

Pea threw down the paper and rushed out to do something he considered unethical but necessary. It was his morning habit to collect the daily papers from the front lobby and deliver them to the ladies, leaving them in the vine decorated metal holders attached to the wall outside their doors. Now, he unfolded Nan's paper and removed the entire *Life and Times* section. Hopefully, Nan knew nothing of the interviews so she wouldn't be looking for her name in print, as the others were sure to do.

Indeed, Maizie and Fiona and Carlotta and Sulie were all waiting for their paper. As he spoke to each in turn, warning her not to say anything to Nan, he watched her reaction carefully to detect if she was the one who had revealed Nan's secret. But they all seemed to be consumed with curiosity to read about Nan. Even Maizie, whom he'd suspected in particular, had snorted, "Nan? What about her? Is she dead? Seems to me it won't hurt if we tell her that." Pea left her muttering in her threadbare bathrobe with *Hilton Arms* written on the back, the chenille worn off in such a way it read *Hilt Ars*.

Pea had hoped one of his ladies would be guilty of this betrayal because that would absolve Lacy. He should have known she'd discover Nan's dilemma, and now he regretted not telling her himself and swearing her to secrecy. Not that that would have been any guarantee.

That afternoon, at the rock, with an early returning pair of Robins in attendance and Lacy looking like spring herself dressed in a yellow car coat, Pea held out the newspaper, the paragraph about Nan circled in red. "I assume you are responsible for this," he said coldly.

"Yes, Pea, and I'm sorry. I realize I probably wasn't supposed to know about Nan."

"But why? Nan will be destroyed when she sees this."

"I thought of that, Pea, I really did. And I thought a long time before I told the reporter. But I did it for the good of the cause, and I think, for Nan as well."

"How is being publicly humiliated going to help her?" Pea was getting really angry. It was an unfamiliar feeling, this energy rising from his mid-section. Unlike the frightened, insulted anger he'd felt toward Mr. Ryan, this was real outrage tinged with grief for Nan and the dismay of someone betrayed. Lacy stared at him, eyes wide, almost in fear. This gave him courage. It shamed him, too, to be emboldened by a woman's fear.

He needn't have worried, for apparently this new Lacy was not one to be cowed for long by male aggression. She stood up and said calmly, "I don't blame you for being upset, Pea. I know I took a chance. If I'd confided in you, you would have forbidden me to speak." A mischievous look came into her eyes. "But you've got to admit it makes compelling human interest."

Yes, this was the old Lacy, but the betrayal of Nan wasn't half-melted chocolate in the pocket of his white dress pants or a cricket in his lunchbox. This was playing with a woman's life. He started to speak but she held up her hand to silence him, taking a step backward before turning to say over her shoulder: "Just you wait and see what comes in the mail. If my hunch is correct, this may be the lever you need to pop Nan out of that apartment."

Chapter Nineteen

Pea collected the morning papers reluctantly, fearing he couldn't say what. He only knew there were forces afoot beyond his control. So far, he'd been the last to know of each new development in the impending demise of Hobarth Manor.

Sure enough, on the front page of the *Life and Times* section was a picture of Maizie and her band of geriatric demonstrators, a collection of stalwarts with canes, wheelchairs, and walkers.

Pea read the accompanying article, based on an extensive interview with Maizie. According to the reporter, this remarkable woman took a woman's prerogative not to reveal her age but admitted to having lived at Hobarth Manor the longest of any of the remaining tenants. This wasn't true, nor was it true Maizie was the driving force, as the paper claimed, behind the effort to have Hobarth Manor placed on the historic register. Nor was she in charge of the upcoming fundraisers to be held at the Art Institute, dates to be announced.

Evidently Maizie had also fielded some questions about the other tenants. To Pea's surprise, she credited Carlotta with being a world-famous concert pianist in her day and she actually mentioned Sulie's famous restaurant. She claimed Nan was a well-known artist before becoming a shut-in, due to her tragic weight gain. And what was poor Nan to do, Maizie was quoted as saying, once the wrecking ball started swinging? Given the positive nature of Maizie's words, Pea suspected Lacy had tutored her.

As the date for Carlotta's concert approached, Mozart and friends stalked the halls of Hobarth Manor from mid-morning to dinnertime, with short breaks for Carlotta's lunch and her mid-afternoon nap. Pea went around humming Mozart's Piano Sonata Number 11, and something else he'd never heard before. A surprise, Carlotta told him when he took up her mail, something new she was adding to her repertoire.

Pea waited for the complaints that Carlotta was exceeding the practice time allotted to her, but with Maize preoccupied with her picket brigade and Sulie and Fiona with their own fundraising projects, no one seemed to notice or care how long Carlotta practiced.

In days to follow, the newspaper ran a series of articles on the ladies of Hobarth Manor. Sulie was pictured holding a scrapbook open to a photograph of herself and her late husband in front of their restaurant. An enterprising reporter had dredged up the newspaper account of Sulie's husband's death, in all its gruesome detail.

Fiona, to Pea's surprise, had invited the press into her walk-in closet, a former extra bedroom Pea had converted when she moved in with five trunks and enough hatboxes to contain her collection of five hundred plus hats, mostly from the 1930s. Pea had built shelves and shoe racks and lined the walls with rods, but he had never seen her collection, which she now so generously opened to the press. She was even shown modeling what was described as "a gown of Andalusion blue satin adorned with twists of peach georgette" with "dyed-to-match satin pumps and long cream kid gloves."

The article contained nothing of real substance about Fiona herself. The most personal detail given was the tearful question Fiona posed at the end of the piece: what would she do with all this if she were forced to move? She could never afford a place with the closet space to which she was accustomed.

Pea noted with relief that so far Leonardo had escaped the attention of the press, but there was a sidebar on Nan, in which the reporter expressed frustration in her attempts to gain access to "the reclusive tenant."

Pea was vigilant in protecting Nan from the press and refused all interviews. He was astonished when a reporter unearthed someone from his old army unit who remembered him for his scalloped potatoes, something Pea himself had forgotten about. Now he wondered if he should volunteer to whip up a platoon-sized batch for the fundraiser.

All this human interest prompted the newspaper's readership to weigh in, and a lively debate ensued in the *Letters to the Editor* section.

An anonymous neighbor described Hobarth Manor as "the most beautiful and most interesting landmark in the neighborhood," and went on to say, "Should it be replaced with what passes for a more sensible use of the land, those of us who drive or walk by it every day will find our lives sadly depleted."

A sympathetic reader responded: "As a society we often disregard our past. That is unfortunate when it's a beautiful old building, tragic when it's our elderly. The ladies of Hobarth Manor apparently have much to offer an uncaring society, but even if they did not, do they deserve to lose their home?"

Another said that after reading the series of articles, she felt she knew the ladies personally and she hoped the owner of Hobarth Manor would "reconsider his decision to deprive Maizie, Sulie, Carlotta, Fiona and Nan of their home." Several correspondents made Pea cringe when they expressed a wish to hear more about "the unique population of Hobarth manor, particularly the reclusive Nan and the elusive Caretaker."

Although no one was cruel enough to say the ladies should be put out on the street, there followed a spate of letters that seemed to disregard their existence.

One so-called expert wrote that it was a mystery how such an architectural monstrosity had so far escaped destruction. In the next issue, another correspondent suggested Hobarth Manor had survived only because the preponderance of architectural detail was so overwhelming, it was impossible to take it all in, thus making the building virtually invisible.

Evidently all the publicity sparked some curiosity as to what, exactly, "preponderance of detail" meant, for subsequent critics obligingly filled in the details.

"Most unusual," one wrote, "are the small caryatids supporting the entablature over the many windows, three on each side of the portico and another row just above. The effect is disconcertingly crowded." Pea felt like pointing out that the marble statues of women were appropriate, given the nature of the building's inhabitants.

"It's a strange mishmash of forms," ran one letter. "The fluted ionic columns with voluted capitals supporting the front portico suggest Greek Revival. The unusual entablature above the portico, with the clean lines of the architrave, also suggest Greek Revival, while the vine leaf frieze it supports is early Gothic." That letter prompted a local wag to suggest the building's proper name should be Mishmash Manor.

Still another commented, "What is one to make of the variation of a Palladian window, or what is more commonly known as a Venetian window, that graces, or, one might say, disgraces, the upper floor? Taken together with all the other details, the eye does not know where to go."

And finally, a contributor came back to what Pea considered the only important point, by writing: "So what if some people consider Hobarth Manor an eyesore? It's the ladies' home. Let it be." Somehow, he knew that to those who held the power, that consideration was of least importance.

Chapter Twenty

Once Pea had made up his mind to persuade Nan to go on a diet, he couldn't bring himself to face her. For days, he tipped the delivery boy to take up her groceries and had even considered calling a meeting of the Hobarth Manor Tenant's Association. After all, this weight thing appeared to be a woman's issue. There were, of course, plenty of fat men on the streets but they didn't appear to be at all concerned about it, and all the before and after pictures in the ads seemed to be of women.

Inspiration came from the cover of a magazine in the supermarket checkout line. "How to lose ten pounds in one week by eating six meals a day," the headline read. That might appeal to Nan. He picked up the magazine, along with three others. One promised instant weight loss with a five-step program involving steak and lots of fruit. Another offered a more intellectual approach: "How to revitalize your willpower center." It showed a picture of an attractive woman sitting cross-legged on a cushion. Behind her was a poster showing a human figure with lines and arrows indicating the head center, the appetite center, and most interesting, the on-and-off switch in the brain. It was beyond Pea, but then he lacked Nan's education.

The third commanded the reader to "Save this house." Superimposed upon the picture of a woman's body was a house, with various levels, each corresponding to a different color. Floating above, in a nebulous cloud, was a detached head with a peaceful, smiling face. Pea found the article inside and learned the woman had exited her body; that is to say, her messy home, while it was being renovated. This was an obvious euphemism for shedding unwanted pounds. Pea became so fascinated with this piece he had to let two people with loaded-down carts go ahead of him while he considered whether the method's spiritual approach would curb Nan's appetite or spark an eating binge. In the end, he bought all the magazines, including a more scientific looking one that promised a breakthrough in diet pills, maybe the most realistic idea of all. Perhaps reading them would keep Nan too busy to snack for a day or two and then she'd be on her way to, as one magazine cover put it, "a new, thinner, revitalized you."

Later that day, when Pea took up the magazines, he was surprised to see Nan's door slightly ajar. He knocked, and she appeared in a paint-smeared smock and fuzzy slippers, her hair pulled back from her face by a plain rubber band and wearing no make-up. She smelled of turpentine and carried a color palette in one hand and a paintbrush in the other.

"Hello Pea," she said with her usual warm smile. "How nice of you to stop by. No, leave the door open. I like to hear Carlotta's music. It inspires me."

Pea mumbled an apology for his neglect.

She waved her paintbrush. "Oh, I know, Pea, we've all been busy, what with all the excitement." She led the way to the living room.

"I brought you some magazines," he said. Embarrassed by the covers, he placed them face down on the table. The usually neat living room was cluttered with canvasses, seascapes similar to those framed on her walls, and some new ones, abstract splashes of color, blues and reds and deep gold. Nan's easel, which Pea hadn't seen out of the closet for years, had been placed under the skylight.

"I'm making a comeback, Pea," she said. "Isn't it exciting? When I looked over these old canvasses, I decided to do something entirely new. Maybe I'll do a retrospective and then contrast it with the new me. What do you think?"

Pea studied the work-in-progress, which did seem oddly in sync with the strains of Mozart floating in from the hall. He found it pleasing to the eye, although he couldn't say why because it wasn't actually of anything.

"I'm calling it 'Breaking Out,'" she said shyly.

"Well, I like it," Pea said. "But you know I'm no expert. It just, well, has a happy feel to it."

She laughed. "Pea, I think I'll let you write the text for my paintings."

Pea left, feeling less anxious about Nan than he had for weeks, although he was disappointed at not having been offered even a stale cookie.

Chapter Twenty-One

"Lacy, where did you find the architect's name?" Pea inquired. He was sitting beside her on their rock and this time he wasn't going to let her go until he got a straight answer.

"From the library. I thought the buildings he designed looked sort of like Hobarth Manor. Parts of them, anyway."

"Why didn't you just look up the records at City Hall?"

"I did, but the clerk couldn't find them. So I improvised."

"You mean you lied."

"Oh, well, I guess. But everybody's been dead for so long, who cares?"

"This person, for one." Pea pulled a letter from his jacket pocket. "It's from Ruby Carthington, a descendent of your architect. She wants to tour Hobarth Manor. She says if it really is her ancestor's work, it's a new discovery, having been left out of the books."

Lacy paled. "But Abel Carthington never married. That's partly why I chose him. I assumed there were no heirs."

"She's his grandniece."

"Oh." Lacy skimmed the letter. "She wants to come next week."

"What are we going to do?" he said.

Lacy thought for a moment, then pocketed the letter. "I'll call her and set up the appointment." Then she reached up and kissed Pea on the cheek. "Don't worry, dear, I'll take care of everything." And she was gone, leaving Pea distracted by the imprint of her lips on his face and the word 'dear' echoing in his head.

Chapter Twenty-Two

Pea sat in a pool of morning sunshine that fell from a high window onto his breakfast table, sipping coffee and sorting through letters to the editor that had appeared in the paper over the past few weeks. He noticed that as time went on, the architecture of Hobarth Manor seemed to be of less interest to his public than his ladies. On the one hand, this was gratifying, but he got nervous when the letters pointed out the bare facts of their existence, as in the first two he read this morning.

"Where are their families?" one correspondent wrote. "Do none of these ladies have children to look after them? I'd be ashamed if my mother was facing eviction with nowhere to go."

And another: "It seems to me the ladies in question are nearing the point where they will no longer be able to live independently. What then? Perhaps it's time for them to face reality and enter proper retirement facilities."

Others proved to be more personal. "What is Fiona's background? She looks familiar. Was she a film star in the thirties?" Pea fidgeted, remembering the wild guesses the other ladies sometimes made concerning Fiona's past. He wondered how long Fiona would be able to dodge the public's curiosity. He realized he was happier not knowing her history.

The next letter was a pleasant surprise. "I believe I heard Carlotta in concert when I was a child. I found an old playbill belonging to my mother with a beautiful picture of her on the cover. Don't we owe it to our artists to treat them better in their declining years?" This one he clipped to give to Carlotta.

And one of Maizie's fans wrote, "I visited the mall the other morning and witnessed Maizie in action. Regardless of what happens to Hobarth Manor, in any future battles I might find myself in, I want her on my side." Pea didn't know whether to be reassured or not by this letter as he still felt anxious every time she set out for the mall.

Maizie's tight curls were dyed red, compliments of an admiring hairdresser at the mall, where she went nearly every morning with her crew of aged activists. While they had initially skated by with a bluff that depended on a security guard's ignorance of the law, it soon became clear to the mall's owners that it would be bad public relations to have the old people removed. Customers loved them. Some even joined the parade of walkers and wheelchairs. It was, by far, the most successful of Lacy's fundraising efforts; although Pea did receive a check in the mail every day or so from readers of the *Life and Times* section of the newspaper.

The last correspondent asked if Nan was really stuck in her apartment. "Does she even exist?" the writer wondered. "Why won't she add her voice to the cause?"

No sooner had Pea put down this letter than the phone rang. It was a sales representative from Weight Watchers, offering Nan a free membership, plus a year's weekly dues in exchange for exclusive rights to before and after pictures.

"That's nice of you," Pea said, "but I don't think Nan would be able to attend your meetings."

"Not to worry," the caller said tactfully. "A local representative will call on her personally, plan her menus, and drop by each week for a weighing-in on Nan's personal scale."

"I don't know if Nan has a personal scale," Pea said. He tried to remember how high the typical bathroom scale went.

"Not to worry. Weight Watchers will furnish that as well."

"I don't know," Pea said, "but I'll ask her and get back to you." In fact, the only drawback to the idea he could see was that he'd have to take the offer to Nan. He decided to get it over with.

Pea had to ring three times before Nan came to the door, wearing the same paint splattered smock and down-at-the-heel slippers. He missed her pretty shoes and carefully made-up face.

"Oh hello, Pea, it's nice to see you." She wandered back into her studio. "Make yourself comfortable," she said vaguely. "I'll take a break soon."

Pea perched uneasily on the sofa and, finding it easier to broach the subject while her back was turned, he outlined the Weight Watchers offer. When he finished, she shook her head, still not looking at him. "I don't think so, Pea."

"But Nan," he said, "Surely you must realize sooner or later you're going to have to…that is, we may lose…Indeed, you may have no choice but to…" How could he say it? And *was* she too big to get through her door? She looked bigger than ever in that smock.

"Yes Pea?" Nan turned, paintbrush poised in the air, dripping bright red onto the floor, where the newspaper spread to protect it had shifted. She blew a strand of hair from her eyes and waited, a distracted smile on her face.

Pea was sweating and his tongue felt as if it were tied in a knot, but at last he got out the dreaded words. "Nan, you may have to lose a few pounds."

She gazed at him uncomprehendingly, red paint still dripping onto the floor. In some corner of Pea's mind, he planned how he would remove the stain from the oak. Fast on the heels of that thought, he asked himself what was the point if the building was just going to be torn down anyway? That drove him to a bluntness he hadn't known he was capable of.

"You may already be too big to get through the doorway. And soon you may have to leave here and I don't know how to help you with this..." He found, to his dismay, he was swallowing back tears. "Now I don't mean to be unkind, Nan, and you understand that to me you are fine just as you are, but we have to have a plan and I know these weight-watcher people can help you if you let them."

Through a teary fog, Pea couldn't tell what effect his words were having, only that Nan continued to stare at him. At least he had her attention. "Please try, Nan," he went on. "I can't fix the door because of the weight-bearing wall and the skylight's no good either because the helicopter might drop you and even if it didn't, you know the newspapers would get wind of it. Someone would call them and even if they didn't, those reporters are always snooping around, and they know things before I hear about them and, well, think about...think about your dignity." He stopped, out of wind and out of material furnished by his nightly worry sessions. He realized then, all the time he'd been speaking, he'd been holding out his hands beseechingly. He looked at them as though they belonged to someone else, then dropped them to his sides in defeat. "I'm sorry, Nan," he said. "Please forgive me."

"Oh Pea," Nan said. "Dear Pea." Don't you see, I don't have time for these people to watch my weight. Why, I can't even find time to bake cookies for you." She brightened. "But I can make you a cup of tea. Or hot chocolate." She put the paintbrush to soak and rummaged in her cupboards. "Oh dear, I'm out of hot chocolate. And the cookie jar is empty. It will have to be tea, I guess."

"Nan, no. That's not what I came for." In spite of her rejection of Weight Watchers' offer, he felt a tremendous relief. He had said the worst possible things to his friend and the floor was still firm beneath his feet. But how could he get through to her?

Nan moved a stack of mail off the kitchen chair and motioned for him to sit. "Nonsense, Pea. I'm being a terrible hostess. I'll make you some toast and jam. I seem to be out of peanut butter, and I hope you don't mind this store-bought bread. I haven't had a chance to bake this week at all."

Pea eyed the stack of mail on the table. He'd noticed lately her box was unusually full, but then all his ladies were getting mail. Carlotta called it her fan mail; Fiona pretended it was an imposition on her time; Maizie seemed to consider it her due, especially those letters containing donations, which she proudly turned over to Pea for deposit.

"Don't you think you ought to open some of these?" he said.

"As soon as I finish this painting," Nan said. "I'll open my mail and pay some bills and clean this place up. That reminds me, Pea, I have an order to be picked up at the art supply store. Canvass for my next painting." She hesitated, then went on in a rush: "Would you believe, Pea, I've already done it in my head. I woke up in the night with a plan, colors and all, for the whole thing. It's been like that, lately. As I finish one thing, the next project just comes to me. Anyway, would you pick up my order?"

Out of frustration Pea considered saying no, telling her she'd have to lose weight, get out of her apartment, and stop being dependent on someone who could barely take care of himself. But he merely nodded, drank his tea, ate his slightly burnt toast, and left Nan to her work.

Chapter Twenty-Three

In the absence of hard facts about Nan, the press resorted to conjecture. She was ill. She had had a heart attack and her apartment had been converted into a hospital room. She was severely depressed and that was why she refused to speak with anyone. A representative of one of the more outrageous tabloids claimed he got as far as Nan's door and was turned back by an armed guard. Was she being held against her will? As far as Pea knew, no reporter had gotten any further than the front door, and even Maizie couldn't have been taken for an armed guard.

He was contemplating the situation when Hattie Allspring, from *Large and Luscious Magazine*, came to his door. Hattie was not only large; she was luscious, with creamy, unlined skin and a cascade of golden hair. She wore a dress the color of violets that flowed gracefully in tiny pleats to her ankles.

Up to now, Pea had turned all reporters wanting interviews away without ceremony, but it occurred to him that this one might help Nan. His first impression was that Hattie had to be as big as Nan, which conjured up an uncomfortable image of her stranded in the hallway with her notepad while Nan was stuck on the other side of the door. The idea was so distressing, he invited Hattie in to see if she would fit through his door. To his relief, she not only made it through, but also managed the steps nicely, teetering gracefully on tiny high heels.

While he made tea, Hattie fanned out several copies of her magazine on the table. The models on the covers were almost as attractive as Nan was on a good day. "Tell me," Pea said, "how you would use Nan's story."

"What I think you are asking, Mr. Jamieson, is 'what is the philosophy of our magazine?' As you know, our culture tends to vilify large people, especially women. *Large and Luscious* celebrates them. All our models are what our society considers overweight. Even obese." She disposed of the word 'obese' with a slight shudder. "We at the magazine take a different view. We demonstrate the true beauty of the individual. And I'm not just speaking of so-called inner beauty, a tired phrase often used as a euphemism for homeliness. It's my personal opinion, and the stated philosophy of *Large and Luscious Magazine*, that no woman has true inner beauty until she accepts how she looks on the outside."

She paused to add two teaspoons of sugar to her tea. "There is no excuse for any woman to be considered, or worse, to consider herself, homely. Or overweight, for that matter. We are what we are, Mr. Jamieson, and during our brief stay on this planet we ought to celebrate that. Whatever it is."

All this sounded a bit idealistic to Pea, although he had long felt Nan was truly beautiful, both inside and out.

"No Pea," Nan said later the same day, when Pea asked if she would see the reporter. "It's very nice of them to think of me, but please tell her I'm much too busy right now."

"It might not be a bad idea for you to speak to her," he said. "You know, set the record straight." He handed her a copy of *Large and Luscious Magazine*. "At least have a look."

"Maybe later, Pea," Nan said. He was grateful she at least didn't seem horrified at the idea. He wondered if she had even bothered to read the newspapers he saw spread out to protect the floor from dripping paint.

He noticed her mail was still unopened. Now, she took the issue of *Large and Luscious Magazine* and, with barely a glance at the pretty woman on the cover, set it aside and went back to putting the finishing touches on an abstract painting vaguely resembling a swan flying out of a skylight.

Chapter Twenty-Four

Pea stood beside Lacy at the window on the second-floor landing and watched a tall, tweedy woman with a briefcase climb out of the taxicab. With her was a portly gentleman who barely came to her chin. She stopped at the end of the sidewalk and stared, open-mouthed, at Hobarth Manor, now and then shaking her head. They clearly were not going to get away with this. The man took out a camera, and at the woman's direction, shot a few pictures, then followed her around the side of the building.

"Why do you suppose she needs pictures?" Pea asked.

"Maybe to compare Hobarth Manor to her uncle's other works?" Lacy said.

His *other* works? Had Lacy lost her hold on reality? But maybe it was best if he too pretended, for the moment, they weren't guilty of fraud.

"We'd better give her whatever she wants," Lacy said, "or we're toast."

Minutes passed before the couple reappeared and marched toward the front door. Pea scurried down the steps to let them in.

The woman ignored Pea's outstretched hand. "Percival Jamieson McNulty, I assume? Ruby Carthington, on behalf of my esteemed great uncle, Abel Carthington. Or I should say," and her well penciled eyebrows rose significantly above horn-rimmed glasses, "I should say, on behalf of my uncle's reputation as one of the great architects of the early twentieth century."

"Yes, well, welcome," Pea said, pocketing the ignored hand. "And you are?" he said to her accomplice.

The man responded by taking his picture. "Joe's the name. How about standing over there by the lady?" He indicated Lacy who stood on the landing above.

"That will do, Joe," Ms. Carthington said. "Save your film for the building." She looked around the foyer, frowning at the stylized lilies on the wallpaper.

Lacy, who had shrunk into the background at the sight of the upraised camera, now stepped forward in the manner of a tour guide. "Note if you will, Ms. Carthington, the light pouring into the building from so many directions. I understand this is one of the qualities; that is, a signature of your uncle's."

"Light. Yes. Light." Ms. Carthington stood reflectively in a mote-filled beam coming through the front door's beveled glass. "But this floor!" She seemed to recoil from the black and white checkerboard marble. "And that wallpaper!"

"Yes, yes, very unusual, isn't it?" Lacy said, as she descended a few steps, keeping one eye on Joe's camera. "I understand the original wallpaper can be seen in the Victoria & Albert Museum. That's in London."

"I'm well aware of the location of the Victoria & Albert Museum," Ms. Carthington sniffed. I'm also aware that the Art Noveau style used in decorating this entry is very unCarthingtonian."

"Perhaps the wallpaper—and the floor—were added later," Lacy said. "But surely you must agree, the Palladian window…"

"A bastardization of a Palladian," Ms. Carthington said, as she peered upward to the arched window illuminating, not only the foyer, but also the second-floor hallways.

This wasn't going well at all. "Perhaps I could offer you some refreshment," Pea said. "If you'll follow me to my apartment…" He indicated the door to the basement.

Ms. Carthington exchanged glances with her cameraman who had made his way to the top of the stairs but now descended, almost at a run. The poor man must be hungry.

"Thank you, yes," she said stiffly, in the manner of one granting Pea a favor by accepting his hospitality.

Ms. Carthington thawed somewhat over Nan's coffee cake, which Pea had made himself. He'd hinted strongly for Nan to provide it, but his distracted tenant was only able to come up with the recipe.

His guest took an unexpected interest in Pea's lifestyle, asking about his childhood in Hobarth Manor and where he'd live if efforts to preserve his home failed. He answered her questions, thinking it couldn't hurt if she developed some sympathy for their cause. She even took a few notes. Meanwhile, Lacy shadowed Joe, keeping out of range of his camera lens. He declined refreshment to take a surprising number of photographs of Pea's apartment.

"Excuse me, Ms. Carthington," Pea said, when he caught a glimpse of Joe peering into his storeroom, "but I don't see much of architectural interest here. Why is he…?"

"He's looking for obscure signature details of my uncle's work," she said. "One never knows when one is going to run across a telling feature. That wainscoting, for example. Notice the detail on the trim along the top. Tiny carvings of pineapple. Most interesting. Joe," she called, "don't forget the wainscoting." Joe bounded in from the living room where he had just finished documenting Pea's display of family photographs.

Having at last exhausted her curiosity about Pea's childhood, Ms. Carthington allowed Lacy to lead the way up the open staircase. She was distracted on the way by the acorn carvings on the balustrade.

"Lovely, isn't it?" Lacy said.

"Interesting," Ms. Carthington mused. "And, I must admit, typical of my uncle's work. Joe?" Snap went the camera.

"As are so many things," Lacy enthused. "The caryatids, the portico, the recessed columns at either end of the building. And if you'll just follow me…"

Pea trailed after the two women as they climbed to the second floor, which was bathed in light, not only from the Palladian, or Venetian, window, but also from a skylight directly above the entryway, and the bay windows at each end of the hallway.

"I understand those oriel windows represent another feature common to your uncle's work," Lacy said. "Also, the broad architrave around the windows on the outside."

Oriel windows? Architrave? Pea wondered where she had learned to talk like that.

"I did take note," Ms. Carthington said. "And yes, there are some features of this building that were often repeated in my uncle's work. But never…" She paused for emphasis. "Never all in the same building."

Lacy smiled with a calm confidence at which Pea could only marvel. "Perhaps Hobarth Manor was a late-in-life piece de resistance," she said, "in which it was his intention to bring everything together under one roof."

Ms. Carthington patted her briefcase. "I have photos of all his known works. From the family archives. And I assure you, there's no such mention anywhere in his writings of such a piece de resistance."

Although Ms. Carthington seemed offended by the worn oriental carpet in the hall, she stood for a long moment, gazing upward at the molding around the skylight, carved from the same wood and in the same style as the staircase, and she seemed to appreciate that the effect was repeated around all the windows. "Capture that detail, please, Joe," she said.

"It's the same in one of the apartments," Lacy enthused. "The occupant is an artist and…"

Pea shot her a warning look, too late.

"Really?" Ms Carthington said. "I should like to see that skylight. Joe? Leave that and come along." She started down the hall. "Is the apartment this way?"

Lacy nodded, avoiding Pea's desperate glance.

"I'm sorry, Ms. Carthington," Pea said, "but I can't possibly disturb this tenant. He trotted to catch up, but Joe had forged ahead and was already knocking on Nan's door.

"Please don't do that," Pea said.

But Nan had already opened the door and before she could say hello, Joe snapped her picture. "Oh," Nan screamed. She tried to close the door, but Joe was too quick for her. He brushed her aside and seemed intent on capturing the apartment's entire contents before he got thrown out.

Ms. Carthington held her hand out to Nan. "Please accept my apologies, Miss. My friend likes to get some human interest in his shots, and he tends to forget our mission here today is to photograph only the building."

"Oh," Nan said, breathless. "You must be Ms. Carthington."

"Please excuse me," Pea said, "But I think the skylight is the only thing here…"

"Obscure details," Ms. Carthington boomed. "One never knows when an obscure detail will turn the tide." She pushed past Nan into the apartment, almost every surface of which was crowded with paintings, some finished and some not, all of which were apparently of architectural interest. "Joe, please," said Ms. Carthington. "Stop wasting your film. Get that archway into the bedroom. No, no, from the other side."

Dozens of camera flashes later, they left a confused and dazed Nan, paintbrush still in hand, standing in her doorway.

"I'm so sorry, Nan," Pea whispered as he followed Lacy and the others out the door. "I tried to stop them."

"I suppose there was no harm done, Pea," she said. "I'm only sorry I didn't have anything to offer your guests." Pea had to marvel

103

at her resilience. Her privacy had just been brutally interrupted and all she could think about was her failure to be a good hostess. And why wasn't she upset at these strangers coming into her apartment when just a short while ago she refused to let in anyone but himself?

At the front door, Ms. Carthington held out her hand. "I will study Joe's photographs, make some comparisons and get back to you. But don't get your hopes up too high." She hesitated before adding, "There is, of course one way to substantiate your claim."

"And that is?" Lacy said.

"The time capsule. My uncle always included one beneath the cornerstone. Perhaps we'll only know for certain if this building is my uncle's work when the capsule is either opened or one is not found. That is, when Hobarth Manor is demolished."

Chapter Twenty-Five

A few days later, Lacy rang Pea's bell, suitcase in hand, bringing the number of ladies under his protection to six. He flinched at the dark bruise that ran from below her left eye to the hollow of her cheekbone. "He did this to you?" Pea took her suitcase and led her to a chair. "What else did he do? Did you call the police? We need to get you to a doctor."

"I'm okay, Pea." She touched her face. "Maybe some ice." She handed him the morning newspaper. "I guess you haven't seen this."

The *Life and Times* section was filled with Joe's photographs. There was Nan standing in her doorway wearing her spattered smock and run-over slippers, without make-up and hair askew, dripping paintbrush in hand. And there was Lacy, too.

"We should have seen it coming, Pea," she said, as he poured her a cup of coffee. "We should have known they were reporters the minute Joe started snooping around your apartment."

"You're right," Pea said miserably. "It's all my fault. I tried too hard to keep the press out. It just made them all the more determined. And now look at you, driven from your home…"

"Not everything that goes wrong in this world is your fault, Pea," Lacy said. "Sometimes I think you have an exaggerated idea of your own importance."

The last was delivered with an offhandedness that shocked him. What did she mean by saying he thought himself important? Surely if he were at all important, he'd have come up with some means of saving their home.

"I suppose we should be relieved that reporter wasn't really Abel Carthington's niece," Lacy said. "And this isn't a bad picture of Nan. As for her paintings, we couldn't have paid for better publicity."

He had to admit she was right. The public was now aware that Nan was not only a very large woman, but also a very talented one, for her artwork was shown to good advantage. But still... something had been bothering Pea about Lacy, something beyond her willingness to manipulate situations and compromise the truth. Now, he listened to her enthusiasm build as she went happily on about the upcoming fundraiser, and he realized what it was. She didn't really see his ladies. He pushed his half-empty cup aside and stood up. "It wasn't Nan's choice," he said.

"What wasn't?" Lacy looked up, genuinely puzzled.

"To be photographed like this." He slapped the paper with the flat of his hand, harder than he intended, which caused Lacy to flinch, leaving him disarmed and confused. "I'm sorry," he said. "You're safe here." He took up the ice pack and fitted it tenderly over her face. "Best keep this on." He thought for a moment. "There's a vacancy on the second floor. Still mostly furnished. Anyway, it should do for now."

Later, when she was settled in, Pea went back to his basement. There, he paced. In spite of what Lacy said, this was his fault, all of it. He'd gone along for the ride, as usual, and now his dear Nan had been compromised. Just once, he wished he could think of some action that would ward off these disasters. Even Lacy, underhanded though she was, at least had courage. Why, she had risked everything to save Hobarth Manor. If she had gotten them into trouble with her dishonesty, then it was his fault for not taking charge.

And another thing. Almost everyone who was involved in this drive to save Hobarth manor was thriving. Nan was painting again.

Carlotta was preparing for a comeback. Fiona and Sulie appeared to be full of plans, although he failed to see how Fiona's sense of style and Sulie's turtle soup was going to save anyone. Even Maizie had found an outlet for her energy. But himself? His days were filled with anxiety. He longed for the time when almost any problem that came up responded to his skills with a hammer and wrench.

But even then…even then, was that what he really wanted out of life? It brought up another question nagging at the back of his mind since this all began. How had he gotten into this position of having to take care of five women? His ladies. Now there were six. Was it his habit of doing nothing that had earned him this responsibility? Was anything in his life of his own choosing? A pain began to spread from his temples to the back of his head. He couldn't think any more about this now.

He'd have to visit Nan, of course, and take the newspaper with him. But that was just more damage control. He could sense still another disaster looming on the horizon. His pacing had carried him into his mother's old sewing room, as if she had directed him there. He stopped before her writing desk to stare at her good Cross pen set, hardly disturbed since her passing. Without thinking, he sat down and took out a sheet of yellowed stationery, some his mother had ordered, with *Hobarth Manor* embossed at the top. Whatever damage the letter he was about to write did to the cause, he would just have to live with.

Chapter Twenty-Six

It was mid-day when Pea next visited Nan. Sun poured in through the skylight of her apartment, onto her latest painting, an abstract in primary colors, drying on the easel. Her usual signature, a small *Nan*, was in the lower right-hand corner.

Nan at her kitchen table wiping away tears as she sorted her mail. He tucked the newspaper inside his jacket. Now wasn't the time for her to see herself portrayed in a paint-spattered smock with no make-up and uncombed hair.

"What is it, Dear?" he said, taking a plump white hand between both of his.

"All these people…letters from…here…" She pulled one from a pile. "This is from Dottie. She's been trapped upstairs in her home for twenty years. Think of it. Twenty years. Her mother brings up all her food. They watch television together and she listens to music and works crossword puzzles. Sometimes friends visit, but not often. Her mother is getting old and it's getting hard for her to manage on the stairs." Nan put down the letter. "This whole stack is like that, from people trapped in their homes." Her voice broke. "Some of them sent money. Here, I made a list of people to thank. Oh, how I wish I could do something for them." She shoved a stack of bills and checks across to Pea.

All this money made Pea nervous. It kept pouring in, not just in correspondence, but in nickels and dimes and bills. Checks, some quite large, written on the spot at the city mall where Maizie relentlessly drove the picketers. What was he to do with it if their efforts to save Hobarth Manor failed, as surely they must?

Nan chose a letter from another pile. "So many people want to help," she said. "Here's one from a woman by the name of Jennie Craig. She wants to send me a year's supply of frozen food. And here's an offer of a free membership to a woman's gym. CURVES, it's called. 'No men, no make-up, no mirrors,' she writes. Have you heard of it? And here's a lovely letter from a man who belongs to something called Overeaters Anonymous. Apparently, it's an organization for people who are addicted to food. Can you imagine?"

Pea shook his head. No, he couldn't imagine it.

Nan sat for a moment, her handsome brow knit into fine lines. Finally, she said, haltingly: "You don't think I got this way because I'm some kind of addict, do you?"

Perhaps it was better to change the subject. "What does he want?" Pea said.

"He says he wants to help me. He sent these pictures of himself, one taken before he lost weight and one after." She shoved them toward Pea. She pointed to the 'after' picture. "He looks like he could use a good meal."

Pea had to agree.

She put the photos back in with the man's letter and tapped the pile it came from. "All these are from OEA members," she said. "A local Chapter offered to hold their meetings here in my apartment until I feel comfortable going out."

"Why Nan, what a good idea," he said. "Are you going to accept the offer?"

"Oh my, no. I barely have space for one large person, what with getting ready for my show." She waved her hand toward the living room filled with paintings. "Besides," she added in a confidential

109

tone of voice, her hand on the stack of letters, as if to keep their writers from hearing what she said. "Suppose they expected me to get up in front of everyone and say: "My name is Nan, and I'm a food add…" She burst into tears. "Oh, I can't even say it."

Pea wanted to tell her it didn't matter if she or any of the others who had written were truly addicted to food. What did that mean anyway? Maybe he was addicted to Nan's bread and pies and cookies. To the delicious smells that used to come from her apartment. His mouth began to water just thinking of her rhubarb pie. And last night he'd been sure he smelled her bread, the aroma filling his bedroom, and he was just bringing his lips to a thick crust dripping with butter when he woke up. He wanted to tell her that, and he wanted to ask her to make him a rhubarb pie, but he was too ashamed of himself for dreaming of food when he should be helping his friend.

He indicated some letters bundled together with a rubber band, wound twice, as if to keep any from escaping. "How about these?"

Nan colored slightly and lowered her voice to a near whisper. "You can't imagine what some people are willing to put into letters, Pea. Offers of marriage from men I don't even know. And, and other kinds of proposals, as if…" she sighed and pushed the packet aside.

Then, brightening, she picked up a letter set apart from the others. "Whenever I get one of those, I take this one out and it sets me right again." She read, somewhat shyly, "I have hanging in my front entry a lovely landscape of Chesapeake Bay that belonged to my late mother-in-law. It wears the plain signature, *Nan*. Could it be the same Nan who lives in Hobarth Manor? If so, I should like you to know your painting has given our family many years of pleasure."

"Imagine, Pea," she said, folding the letter carefully. "This one doesn't mention my weight at all."

Feeling weak with discouragement and driven by food cravings, Pea left Nan to start her new painting and walked five blocks to a new bakery he'd seen advertised in the paper.

CHAPTER TWENTY-SEVEN

Pea was astonished to see his letter on the front page of the *Life and Times* section under a headline: "The Elusive Percival Jamieson McNulty Breaks His Silence." Above were two photographs, the one printed earlier of him raking leaves and the other taken at the Art Institute in his new suit. It occurred to him that they looked like before and after shots. Before, when life was simple, and after, when it was not.

"At least they found a good picture of you," Lacy said grudgingly. She was sitting on his floor, surrounded by piles of clothing, sorted and neatly folded. She'd been helping him go through his mother's things when the paper came, and her first reaction had been resentment that he'd taken some action without first consulting her.

"Dear Editor," Pea's letter began. "It has come to my attention a mistake was made concerning the architect of Hobarth Manor. It's quite possible it was not Abel Carthingon, after all. Nobody seems to know who designed it, not even City Hall. But it's a nice old building and my father and I have taken good care of it, and it is home to five ladies who have lived here for many years and I don't see that it should matter whose idea it was to build it. I'd just like to set the record straight and thank everyone who has come out for our side and apologize for any confusion this may have caused."

"It's not a bad letter," Lacy conceded, "but we might have gotten by with it. It can't hurt to have people think there was a famous architect involved."

"Let's get one thing straight, Lacy," Pea said. "Nobody around here is going to 'get by' with anything. Do I make myself understood?"

She looked startled. He half expected her to storm out of his apartment and wash her hands of the whole business. Instead, she stared at him for a moment, then gave a strange little smile and said, meekly: "Yes, Pea."

Emboldened, he added: "And any decisions to be made concerning my la…that is, the residents of Hobarth Manor, will be made only after consulting them. Is that clear?"

She shrugged, looking defeated, so unlike her.

He'd made his point, but somehow it didn't feel right, maybe because the bruise on her face hadn't entirely faded. He considered the apartment upstairs she was trying to make look like home. With the help of a sympathetic neighbor, she'd retrieved a few things from the home she'd escaped from: clothing, a couple of lamps, and bedding, along with some cash she'd kept hidden. But the walls were bare. "Lacy," he said, why don't you go to the attic and look around at the wall hangings stored there. Choose whatever you want, and I'll put them up.

Chapter Twenty-Eight

As it turned out, the Art Institute would not be available for the fundraiser, which was now less than two weeks away. Pea's first reaction was relief, as he feared the whole enterprise was inclined to raise false hopes and put off dealing with the inevitable. It was now mid-April, and they might have to be out by mid-July.

"I know what this is about," Lacy said at the emergency meeting of the Hobarth Manor Tenant's Association. "Bertram has brought pressure to bear on the Art Institute's Board of Directors."

"Look," Pea said. "It's time we faced facts." He picked up the morning paper and pointed to the picture of a politician who had announced he was running for Congress. "This is Walker Knolls. When I went down to the office of Myers, Myers, and Fox, there was a picture on the wall with your husband's arm around him. And it says here this Knolls is on the zoning commission. We can get all the contributions and public sympathy in the world, but we have no power. I'll bet Bertram is pals with all those guys on the zoning commission."

"I thought you were in charge of finding out where the bodies are buried," Maizie said to Lacy.

"The what?" Pea said. She was getting more and more frail, at times using the walker when in the past she would have picked it up and carried it. Was her mind going as well?

"Bodies. Bodies. You know, blackmail fodder. At least one of those old boys must have a past that reeks. It's just a matter of finding out." She gave Pea a look of patience reserved for the feeble-minded.

"I hate to say it," Lacy said, "but if there are any bodies around, Bertram is likely to know where they are buried, and he wouldn't hesitate to use them. But that doesn't mean we should give up." Pea found the brave lift of her chin even more touching for her bruised face, which had turned a yellowish purple. There was one body, he thought, Lacy's bruises, in the history of her marriage to Bertram Fox. Not that displaying it to the public would do them any good.

"But what's next?" Carlotta said. "I've already made up the program for my concert." She was close to tears.

"What about my dinner?" Sulie chimed in. "We've ordered napkins with the words *Snapper Stew* printed on them. And the chef at the Golden Bowl? He remembers eating at our place as a boy. He offered me the services of his assistant for the evening. We've been working on the menu."

"What about all those merchants at the mall who promised me they'd display our flyers?" Maizie said.

"At least we haven't had them printed," Lacy said. "I was going to do that this afternoon."

"And the mannequins," Fiona put in.

"The what?" Pea said.

"Mannequins. For my gowns. The manager of Lawson's has offered some old mannequins from the department store basement."

"Don't forget who's responsible for that," Maizie said. Before Fiona could fill them in, she hurried on. "I got into a conversation with a saleslady at the mall and I told her about Fiona's old rags, and she put me in touch with the manager."

"Yes. Thank you, Maizie," Fiona said stiffly.

"We were going to display them in the same area as Nan's paintings," Lacy said, "and hold a silent auction for both the clothing and the paintings."

Silence fell on the group as they considered how hard Nan had worked to get ready for the show and the fact that now there was no one present to speak up for her. Pea was suddenly filled with regret that the fundraiser was not to come off.

Lacy brightened. "Why not hold the fundraiser here?"

"But we have no dining room," Sulie moaned. "My apartment certainly won't hold a crowd."

"And where would my audience be seated?" Carlotta said. "And Nan's paintings? Where would we hang them?"

"In her apartment, of course, Lacy said. "Why, Nan herself would be a major draw. You know how curious everyone is about her."

Maizie looked thoughtful. "You know, Lacy may be onto something. We could even sell tickets to see Leonardo."

"It's out of the question," Pea said, barely able to contain his anger at having Nan mentioned in the same breath as Leonardo. "We have to protect Nan from the public eye." He stood up, vaguely aware he was clenching his fists. "I don't even want people milling about outside her apartment." For all her crudeness, Maizie was right. The general public would see Nan and Leonardo as part of the same freak show. As long as he was around, that would not happen.

"And it still doesn't solve the problem about the dining room," Sulie said.

"And my audience," Carlotta said.

Pea sat down, dismayed. They were behaving as if he hadn't even spoken.

"Details," Lacy said. "Just details. We could work it all out. And about Nan, Pea. Why not ask her?"

"Indeed, why not?" came a voice came from the doorway. It was Nan, holding a plate of oatmeal cookies, and from the delicious smell tickling Pea's nose, they were still warm from the oven.

They all stared as Nan placed the cookies on the table and turned gracefully on tiny patent leather pumps. She was wearing an ankle length black crepe dress with tiny pleats running the length of the sleeves and from the shoulders to the hem.

"I didn't want to say anything before," she said, "but I've been working my way through my old clothes, gradually getting into smaller sizes. And this morning I tried on this dress and remembered the last time I wore it was to a concert." Her eyes filled with tears. "It made me realize how much I've missed the world outside my apartment." She gave a shaky laugh. "I said to myself, 'Nan, you know that concert wasn't held in this apartment.' So here I am. Ask me."

Chapter Twenty-Nine

As Pea opened his morning paper, he bit into a perfectly fresh, reasonably moist donut from Fred's Pastry Boutique that may as well have been made of sawdust. Once again, Hobarth Manor had made the news. Beneath a picture of Walker Knolls was the caption: "Zoning Commission head running for legislature doubts there's a future for neighborhood treasure. See page one, *Life and Times* Section." And in a box on the lower right-hand corner: "Is a Hobarth Manor resident connected to the underworld?"

Inside, Pea found a reprint of the first picture the paper ran of his building: the uniformed doorman helping a woman with a big, feathered hat out of a 1930s Cadillac. This time, the image of the woman was blown up, and the caption ran, "Could this be Fancy Fiona?" It seemed 'Fancy Fiona' had been the society girlfriend of Bullet Tolson, bootlegger-turned-racketeer who died in prison in the late 1950s.

According to the paper, Fiona had been born into Boston society, but her family disowned her after she took up with the gangster. Pea put down the newspaper, wishing, not for the first time in the past weeks, he were a drinking man.

Outside, he ran into Maizie, who kept her ride to the mall waiting at the curb while she gloated over "that snooty Fiona getting her comeuppance. And in public, too," she added. She clutched her *Save Hobarth Manor* sign and leaned on her walker. She used it a lot now, and not just for show. Pea was still trying to get used to her curly red hair. He noticed she was wearing rouge now, no doubt compliments of her beautician friend at the mall. He listened for as long as he could before interrupting. "Maizie, I want you to promise me you won't gossip about this. If anyone asks, just tell them what a fine woman Fiona is."

"Fine woman. With her airs?"

Pea relieved Maizie of her sign and marched her to the waiting van filled with senior activists. "Listen," he said, "you don't want anything to undermine your efforts to save this place, do you?"

"Well, if you ask me, the publicity is good for us," she said. "And who cares if Miss Snooty Pants gets embarrassed. Or worse."

"I care," Pea said, his hand on the walker and his face near hers. "And if I hear you've so much as implied this news story is true, I'll personally put you out on the curb, Leonardo and all."

A pale and chastened Maizie climbed into the van, and it took at least ten minutes for Pea to feel ashamed for threatening an old lady.

He supposed he should alert Fiona to this unwanted publicity, but he told himself it was too early to knock on her door. He would weed the flowerbeds first. He was busy with this when a taxi pulled up and a man got out with a newspaper under one arm. The stranger wore a plaid tailored suit with wide lapels. A yellow silk handkerchief poked out of his jacket pocket. Were those spats on his feet?

"You must be Mr. McNulty," the man said. The offered hand was soft with long, slender fingers. "I understand you have a tenant here by the name of Fiona! A real classy broad; that is, uh, lady." He indicated Fiona's picture in the newspaper.

"You know her?" Pea said doubtfully.

The man chuckled. "Fiona and I go way back. But see, I don't wanna shock her or anything. Maybe you could tell her I came calling. She can decide if she wants to see me." He handed Pea a card. "Mitch Sanders, Retired," was all it said. No phone number or address, as if the card itself had been retired from any practical function.

Pea took in the slicked black hair, what was left of it, the ruffled shirt, and the stickpin in the wide paisley tie. Did Fiona need protection from this man? Given Mr. Sanders's frailty and uncertain balance, Pea thought he might be up to it if that were the case.

"How about if you give the old girl a jingle?" Mitch said. "I'll just wait here." He sank down on the circular bench. "Give the old bones a rest."

"Fiona," Pea said, when she answered the phone. "Do you know a Mitch Sanders?" The silence on the other end was so intense Pea thought for a moment they had been disconnected. "Fiona?"

There was a quick intake of breath, then a wary: "Why do you ask?"

"He's here. Waiting on the bench outside."

He heard the phone drop on the floor and realized she'd pulled the cord too far in order to see out the window. "Are you sure that's Fingers...er...Mr. Sanders?"

"That's what he says. Shall I send him up?"

"No...yes. But you come with him, Pea. Just give me ten minutes. I've been dressing mannequins all morning, and I'm still in my robe."

Before she could hang up, Pea said: "Fiona, have you seen today's paper?"

"No, why?"

"Never mind."

Fiona answered the door dressed in loose slacks of soft white wool, a green cashmere sweater with shoulder pads, a long necklace of amber beads, and alligator pumps. Except for the black hair framing her face in finger waves, she resembled an aging Katherine Hepburn.

"Fancy, you ain't changed a bit," Mr. Sanders said. "You always was a class act. Didn't I say that, Mr. McNulty?"

"Fingers...er...Mitch," she said, coloring. "How did you know I was here?"

Mitch drew the newspaper from the inside pocket of his jacket and held it out to her. "Imagine my surprise," he said. "First, I see old Walker Knolls on the front page. Remember him, Fiona? Of course, it was "Sneezy" then, on account of his allergies. Then I see what old Sneezy's been up to and who do I find but you, Fancy? It was like old home week."

Fiona took the paper. "Sneezy's running for higher office? Oh my. The underworld? Me?" She quickly flipped to the *Life and Times* section and began to read, forgetting for the moment her visitors were still standing in the hallway.

Seeing that Fiona's visitor meant no harm, Pea began a soft retreat. Halfway down the hall, he heard her say, "Please come in. You too, Pea," she called out sharply. He sighed and made his way back to her door.

With a dozen mannequins dressed in formal gowns arranged about the living room, Pea felt as if he were entering a very quiet cocktail party. An open archway revealed another group seated around the dining room table. They were decked out in afternoon dresses, travel suits, and evening wear, with one in what appeared to be a 1920s bathing costume. The door to the spare bedroom Pea had years ago converted into a walk-in closet stood open, exposing more figures in various postures and stages of undress. Several were stacked in one corner, naked arms and legs protruding, waiting for Fiona to work her magic on them.

"Sit down, please," Fiona said distractedly, not seeming to notice the mannequins had all the seats.

"Allow me," Pea said, after an awkward moment. He picked up a mannequin dressed scantily in amber silk and deposited her on a dining room chair, thinking it would be nice if his ladies were so easily managed.

"I'll help you, old boy," Mitch said, following him with another.

At last, they were all seated, Fiona in a chair and the two men on opposite ends of the sofa with a mannequin seated in the middle. They looked like nervous suitors who knew they didn't stand a chance with the haughty fashion plate between them.

"So. You're here." A confused Fiona laughed nervously as she swept the room with a heavy braceleted arm. "You must be wondering about all this." She sounded gracious, but Pea could tell she was upset by the way she carried herself, as if she could rise above the situation by making herself taller.

"Oh no," Mitch said. "I've spent most of my life avoiding explanations. They only tend to incriminate, you know, and what I don't know nobody can hold me accountable for."

"It's for a fashion display," she said. "And a silent auction."

"Yes, I don't imagine they'll have much to say," Mitch said in apparent seriousness.

Fiona smiled wanly. "If the clothes could speak...of course it will be sad to part with my gowns, but I have so little need for them now." She indicated the figure on the sofa dressed in a teal blue backless evening gown with a halter-top. "That's Stehli silk," she said. "Perfect for the bias cut, so popular in the thirties."

"I wouldn't know about that," Mitch said, but I think I remember seeing you dolled up in that dress and I have to say I always held a bias in your favor. If you don't mind my saying so, Fancy, you filled that dress out better than that wooden doll."

Fiona drew herself up, aiming for dignified severity, but Pea could tell she was flattered by the words spoken by her old friend. If, in fact, that's what he was. Pea couldn't get a handle on whether or not this Mitch Sanders posed a threat to Fiona. There was something familiar about him, but that could be from watching old gangster movies on television.

The air was heavy with things unsaid, and Pea wondered how long the two of them could hold out. Finally, Fiona gave in. "What exactly brings you here, Mitch?" she said.

"Why, you didn't think I could stay away once I knew you was here, did you?"

"When, uh, did you get...that is, when did they..."

"Let me out?" he said. "About five years before the old man died. Good behavior. Something I'm afraid he didn't get credit for, rest his soul. I visited him, you know, not long before the emphysema and all took him."

"As did I," Fiona said softly, with a quick glance at Pea.

"Yeah, yeah. You always was loyal, I'll say that for you. Not like some. The old man knew it, too. That's why he took such good care of you."

"Perhaps I should go and let you two reminisce," Pea said. He wasn't at all sure he wanted to know any more than he did about Fiona's mysterious past, although he fully intended to question Mitch at some point about Walker Knolls.

"You better stay and hear this," Fiona said. "If Mr. Sanders is here for the reason I think he is, there may be trouble."

"Not a bit of it, Fancy," Mitch said with a hurt expression. "Like the old man, I'd go a long way to keep you out of it. Anyway, the statute of limitations ran out a long time ago."

The Katherine Hepburn shoulders came down a good inch worth of relief, but she was obviously still concerned. "You may as well know, Mitch," she said carefully, with a quick glance at Pea. "There's nothing left. Just a little investment return for rent and food and the occasional hat."

"Now Fiona, I didn't come around to put the finger on you or hit you up for anything other than maybe a promise to do the town with me one of these days. I've got my own thing going, you know. Legit, mind you," he reassured Pea, holding both hands up as if to show they were empty of any incriminating activities. "Straight as an arrow, that's me. No, Fancy, I just came as an old friend to tell you if you need a place to stay, well, I don't mean nothing out of line, you know, but I've got a sweet set-up in an okay neighborhood and if I take out the pool table there'll be plenty of room for your things. Well, maybe not them." He chuckled, indicating the silent cocktail guests. Having said his piece, he nervously wiped his hands on his thighs.

Throughout the last part of Mitch's gallant speech, Fiona had sat wide-eyed, with her mouth slightly open, so Pea wondered if she had heard one word of his generous offer. When Mitch had finished, she rose and paced the room, stopping finally before the two men on the sofa.

"Am I given to understand nobody is looking for me?" she said. "Not that there ever was any reason, of course, you understand." This last was directed at Pea. "The lawyer just showed up one day and informed me I would receive a check every month."

"Louie," Mitch said.

Fiona nodded briefly. "Yes. Louis."

Mitch shook his head sadly. "Poor Louie. The good news is that's all water under the bridge." He looked aghast for a moment. "No offense, of course, given how Louie met his end."

"Of course not, Mitch dear," Fiona said, causing her admirer to beam as if the queen had just knighted him. She perched on the arm of her chair. "I'm really in the clear?"

"Clear as the driven, uh, clear as day," Mitch said.

"And I can go home to Boston?"

"Go anywhere you like," Mitch said. "You're free as a bird."

"You're leaving?" Pea said. He should be relieved, he knew, to be free of some responsibility, but instead he felt as if some part of himself was about to fly away.

"Oh my, no, Pea. I've been dead to my people for too many years. It's just nice to know I could go back if I wanted."

"So, this is all true?" Pea said, holding up the newspaper.

Fiona adjusted a shoulder pad and briefly scanned the rest of the piece. "More or less," she said. "You're sure about that statute-of-limitations thing, Mitch?"

"Cross my heart and hope to die," Mitch said.

Fiona studied the photograph, a smile playing about her mouth and a faraway look in her eyes. "Bullet was so fond of that car. And you know, I still have that hat. And those shoes." She left the two men sitting among the wooden ladies and disappeared into the closet, reappearing several minutes later wearing the feathered picture hat and a mysterious smile. "I'll bet we could get a good price for this," she said, "if we label it 'Bullet Tolson's favorite hat.'"

Chapter Thirty

Pea had taken to watching for Maizie's daily return so he could carry her black purse while she hobbled up to the door with the walker. Today, however, she didn't show up at the usual time. Instead, he got a call from the hospital. She had collapsed at the mall. They were running tests, but it looked like a heart attack, and did he know how to get in touch with her family? That would be, he guessed, the ungrateful daughter.

Pea had never entered any of his ladies' apartments without their permission, but this was an emergency. He left the door open. Somehow that made it seem less an invasion of privacy. It also helped with the fishy odor coming from the spare bathroom.

He started with the rolltop desk on the wall opposite the door, not sure where to begin in the rat's nest of clutter, his hands shaking in his haste to find the phone number.

"Is anything wrong, Pea?" It was Sulie standing hesitantly on the threshold. She was dressed in green corduroy pants and a tattered orange sweatshirt with an indeterminate food stain on the front.

"Do you remember the name of Maizie's daughter?" he said.

"The ungrateful one?" she said. "What do you need her for?"

"Maizie's in the hospital. They think it's her heart. I need to get down there." He emptied a pigeonhole of yellow Post-its covered with Maizie's crabbed handwriting. "She must have an address book here somewhere," he muttered. "Blast, I don't even know what I'm looking for. Was her daughter married?" He emptied the last pigeonhole and started on a drawer.

"Ugh, what a mess," Sulie said, peering over his shoulder. "Look, Pea, you go on to the hospital. I'll go around and ask the others if they remember a name, then come back here and have a look." He shook his head and continued his search into the bowels of Maizie's desk, forgetting about Sulie until the sound of her voice brought him to attention.

"That's no regular alligator." She was standing in the doorway of Maizie's spare bathroom. "Come have a look, Pea. Leonardo is a big old alligator snapping turtle."

The creature lay completely submerged in a bathtub lined with fine screening, the edges of which hung over the side. From the smell, it was time for Maizie's man to come and change the water, or whatever it was he did to keep Leonardo's habitat livable. The smell, however, was nothing compared to the sight of the prehistoric looking creature rising slowly to the surface. It was about two feet long, with three large ridges running the length of its horny shell, a large diamond shaped head, and a thick, rat-like tale. It had a pointed snout with piggish nostrils and short legs ending in vicious looking claws. Its eyes, located on the sides of its head, were surrounded by a star-shaped arrangement of flesh that resembled eyelashes. It blinked, then opened its cavernous mouth to reveal a wormlike tongue moving back and forth.

Pea jumped back, but Sulie stood her ground. "He's hungry," she said. She stepped closer to get a better view.

"Do be careful," Pea said. "Remember what happened to your husband." He had a vision of Sulie with missing fingers. And then what would he do?

"Don't worry, Pea," she said. "Alligator snapping turtles have no flexibility in their necks. Leonardo would have to turn completely around in that bathtub to even get a good look at me and he's gotten too big for that. The one that did in poor Reynolds was the turtle in a big tank. You know, Pea, I think it's true, what they say about pets and their owners growing to look alike." An unnecessary observation, as far as Pea was concerned.

The turtle splashed water over the edge of the tub, turned slowly as far as it could, then gently sank to the bottom, as if to say its audience with these strange beings, who obviously weren't going to feed him, was over.

"The poor thing should have been taken out of there years ago," Sulie said. "Or better yet, put out of its lonesome misery." She turned for one last look. "He must be at least fifty pounds," she mused. Then she muttered, more to herself than to Pea: "Could be tough."

Pea ushered Sulie out and closed the door behind them. He silently cursed himself for having turned a blind eye all these years to what went on in Maizie's spare bathroom. Keeping an alligator snapping turtle had to be illegal. The fundraiser was only days away, when the place would be crawling with strangers.

"What are we going to do?" He couldn't believe he was asking Sulie for advice, but she clearly was in a take-charge mood. And Maizie had to be looked after.

"Turtles have to eat," she said, "and Maizie's not here to feed him, so I'll get him some lettuce. You go on to the hospital. Give me the key and I'll lock up when I'm through."

Pea didn't see his way clear to any other course of action. "Just be careful. Don't get too close to that thing." As he left, he could hear Sulie mumbling to herself as she rummaged through Maizie's refrigerator looking for greens to feed Leonardo.

Chapter Thirty-One

A monitor above the hospital bed ticked along with comforting regularity, but Maizie kept her eyes closed, as if opening them was beyond her strength. "My purse," she whispered. Oxygen hissed through a tube attached to her nose. Pea was overwhelmed with regret. For what, he couldn't have said. But surely, he should have saved her from this.

"I've got it," Pea said. He held up the faded leather bag with its tarnished clasp. Maizie, he observed, had no eyelashes, an uneasy reminder of the star-like arrangement of flesh around Leonardo's eyes. There were deep creases on either side of her nose from her glasses, which lay on the bedside table. Her thick eyebrows were smudged with eyebrow pencil and the only other color left to her face was two dots of pink rouge. Her permed hair, red except for a touch of grey at the roots, lay like damp corkscrews on her pink scalp. Skin hung loose on the arms protruding from a hospital gown. She was tethered to a saline drip, her blue veined hands stuck with needles. Maizie was trapped, at the mercy of those around her, even the ungrateful daughter, he supposed, once she was located. Pea hated to think what that woman would do once she saw Leonardo.

"Open it," she wheezed.

He opened the purse to the usual handful of checks and cash she had greeted him with each day when she returned from the mall. Donations from shoppers and shopkeepers who cared enough to want to help Maizie save her home.

"The day's take," she managed. "Don't forget to write it down." At each meeting, she had proudly presented a running total. No one, he realized, had put in as much effort to save their home. In the end, it had been too much for her.

Pea snapped shut the purse. "Ill be sure to give a full account to the others," he said, his voice breaking. He pulled his chair closer and took a deep breath. "Right now, I have to know where to find your daughter."

"Winifred," she whispered, opening eyes that had lost their usual brightness.

Pea jotted down the name. "Is she married?" he said. "What's her last name?"

Maizie closed her eyes and shook her head. "Who... right mind... would marry...that one?"

But someone had married you, he thought, something he had trouble imagining. "Winifred Dillard, then. How about a phone number?"

"Don't," Maizie said. She gestured toward her purse. "Not... Call...Winston. There...side pocket...card."

Pea fished out a card that said "Winston Morgan, General Repairs. Aquatic Services. No Job Too Small." Or reptile too big, he thought. Winston had come and gone from Hobarth Manor for years, and now Pea felt like kicking himself for not cornering him years ago to insist he reveal the true nature of Maizie's mysterious pet. But then, he hadn't really wanted to know.

Under the circumstances, Pea thought it better not to tell Maizie Leonardo was temporarily in Sulie's custody.

Chapter Thirty-Two

Winston had left a message on his answering machine that he'd be out of town for a week, and although Leonardo seemed to be thriving under Sulie's care, Pea still worried about her getting too close to the creature. He'd breathe easier once Winston took over.

Meanwhile, it was now the day before the fundraiser. Pea had his hands full scavenging chairs and small tables and moving Fiona's mannequins from one corner of the building to the other while she dressed and undressed them and considered the effect of light and shadow on her creations.

Before going off to the hospital to visit Maizie, he carried a card table up to the foyer where he was momentarily startled by a mannequin. She wore a leather coat and had a large envelope handbag tucked under one arm. Her wide-brimmed hat was described on a nearby pedestal table as "Bullet Tolson's Favorite Hat." Earlier that week, pictures of the gangster's trial had appeared in the Baltimore Sun along with several photos of Fiona and Bullet exiting the theater or in elegant nightclubs. Inspired, Fiona had brazenly labeled a number of the outfits with hints they had been touched by the underworld.

"Looks real, doesn't she?" Lacy said, who appeared with a shoebox overflowing with bits of paper. Lacy's bruises were nearly faded, and she appeared to have put on a few pounds since Pea had first seen her several months ago. Her fingernails, which had been bitten to the quick, were growing out. Dressed in jeans and a sweatshirt, she seemed both younger and older than she had then, when he couldn't decide if she looked like an abused wife or a bewildered child.

She put the shoebox on the card table. "I found a stamp for the general admission tickets. Ten dollars will buy a serving of Sulie's fish soup and key lime pie, plus entrance to Carlotta's concert, Nan's Art Gallery, and Fiona's Closet."

Pea noticed she had arranged two stacks of paper slips, one blue and one yellow.

"Why two different colors?"

"That's something special Sulie's cooking up. I thought we could charge $5.00 extra for it. This morning she gave me this sign to display." She propped up a crudely printed cardboard sign reading *Try a sample of Sulie's famous snapper stew. While supplies last.*

Filled with a sudden dread, Pea did a double take. "Lacy, what does this mean?"

"Apparently that chef's assistant came through with fresh turtle meat. I'm thinking I can make a better-looking sign. Why Pea, where are you going?"

Pea took the stairs two at a time. No, it wasn't possible, but the hairs standing up on the back of his neck told him it was. He arrived out of breath at the open door to Maizie's spare bathroom. Sulie was poised on the edge of the bathtub. Leonardo's jaws were clamped around the wooden stick she he'd seen displayed in her apartment. Three inches in diameter and a foot long, it was covered with teeth marks left by generations of snapping turtles.

Pea was afraid to move or speak for fear of distracting Sulie and putting her in the way of those powerful jaws. He could only watch while she drew a sharp knife across Leonardo's throat. Blood pooled in the water and the turtle's body sank while its diamond shaped head on the floor stared up at Pea.

"It's all in the wrist," Sulie said, with a benign smile.

Chapter Thirty-Three

On one of Pea's forays through his storeroom, he had unearthed the green and white striped awning that harkened from the days when Hobarth Manor had a doorman. A bit faded, it was otherwise intact and now in place. In his opinion, the uniformed mannequin standing at attention was a bit over the top, but he held his peace. Lacy had gone to a lot of trouble to procure the male figure and the uniform.

From the sidewalk could be seen three of Fiona's mannequins gazing out of the second-floor Venetian window. The one in the center was dressed in a deep green taffeta gown with a purple sash. To her left was a lady in black with a low neckline. The third figure wore a graceful bias-cut gown in silver lamé. The trio was backlit from inside and graced on the outside by the fruit and vine-leafed frieze above the large three-part windows and the thirty-six marble ladies that flanked the smaller windows.

Lacy had predicted that anyone passing by who saw the mannequins would be unable to resist coming in. Apparently, she was right. By early evening, Hobarth manor was filled with paying guests.

In the foyer, they were greeted by strains of Mozart and the delicious smell of turtle soup drifting down from the upper floor.

Those who hadn't already purchased tickets from Maizie got them now from Lacy, who was stationed at her linen-draped card table. Fiona had dressed her in a black crepe dress with a pale pink pleated sash. Diagonal pleats on the bodice blossomed into ruffles at the left shoulder. Her hair was no longer the same mousy brown worn in a careless ponytail but hung in shiny chestnut waves over her shoulders. She wore a black picture hat trimmed with pink wax flowers. Pea felt almost shy in her presence.

A slotted shoebox near the mannequin wearing Bullet Tolson's favorite hat overflowed with scribbled bids for the silent auction. Fiona had parked a vintage-clad mannequin in every available corner of the building, each with a pedestal table with a box for bidding tickets.

Opposite Lacy's table, an easel held a hastily put together altar consisting of pictures of Maizie chosen from a photo album found in her closet. They were mounted on poster board, and at the center was a tribute, which credited her with contributing the most to the cause of saving Hobarth Manor, sacrificing even her life in the end. Featured in the center was a smiling Maizie leaning on her walker at the mall, surrounded by her faithful followers from the senior center. A huge bouquet of flowers sent over by a florist at the mall rested on the floor nearby. Lacy had wanted to include a donation box, but Pea had insisted they stop with a discreet notice announcing the time and place of a memorial service with a suggestion that in lieu of flowers, donations be made to the Hobarth Manor fund. This had been Maizie's last request, along with her entreaty to Pea that Leonardo be allowed to live out his remaining days in his bathtub. He'd promised, with crossed fingers, since Leonardo had done just that.

The entire picketing brigade was in attendance. Dressed by Fiona in 1930s finery, they were seated strategically throughout the building with donation boxes.

Wearing his new suit, Pea drifted about, shyly greeting guests and checking in on his ladies to see if they needed anything.

Inside her crowded apartment, Sulie held court in purple silk bellbottom trousers, a loose-fitting pink sweater with a draped cowl neckline, and snakeskin shoes, all compliments of Fiona. Her white hair was cut in a fashionable bob. While her assistant watched over the kitchen, Sulie proudly served up turtle soup in paper cups, handing out napkins printed with *The Snapper Stew* beneath a line drawing bearing an uncomfortable resemblance to Leonardo's profile. Out of respect for Maizie, and at the risk of hurting Sulie's feelings, Pea turned down a serving.

Carlotta, at her piano, was dressed in her signature black, this time a corded-silk evening suit consisting of a hip-length fitted jacket with padded shoulders worn over a long, flared skirt. The bunioned feet working the pedals were clad in silver kid sandals, the only thing Fiona could find that came close to providing the comfort of Carlotta's slippers. Pea noted with satisfaction every available chair was taken up with guests enjoying both the music and Sulie's key lime pie, served out of Carlotta's kitchen by one of Maizie's volunteers.

A mannequin outside Fiona's apartment held a placard reading *Fiona's Closet*. Inside, Pea found Fiona working a room crowded with visitors and mannequins. She was dressed in a forest green evening suit with a hip-length fitted jacket, wide shoulder pads, and tight sleeves. A large cream silk bow rested at the high, collarless neckline. A calf-length tulip skirt, long cream kid gloves, and a green felt beret completed the ensemble.

The closet itself had been nearly emptied and now contained a small round table with two chairs. The table was covered to the floor with a white cloth. In the center was a bottle of wine and two crystal goblets. Nearby, a male mannequin in black tie held a dance pose with a lady wearing a flaming red silk gown with full-length gloves and matching pumps.

"You must remember I was brought up in Boston by a very protective family," Fiona was saying. "I had been out only a few months when we met. I was overwhelmed by Mr. Tolson's charm and his good looks. I suppose, given his background, he was taken with the notion of having a debutante on his arm." She paused before a mannequin dressed in a blue taffeta dress with short puff sleeves and covered buttons down the front. Gazing into the distance, she said: "I wore this afternoon dress the day we met. I was visiting an aunt in Baltimore, and I got lost on a shopping trip downtown. Bullet hailed a taxi for me, then climbed in, saying he wanted to make sure I got home safely. He was like a father in that way. Of course, I had no idea how he earned his money until the trial. I was so very young, you know, and he was older."

Her final sentence was delivered with a dismissive wave of her hand as if to say all that no longer mattered. Then she moved to another mannequin in a peach satin gown with three-quarter-length sleeves and a long skirt slit up to the thigh. "Now this dress…"

Pea smiled to think how secretive Fiona had always been. No doubt the others would now have to compete with her for the floor during their meetings. Not that tonight's success was any guarantee they'd be staying in Hobarth Manor. He checked his watch, feeling a stir of excitement. If Mitch were successful, they would soon know if there was any hope at all. He had to be getting back to the foyer, but first he would check on Nan.

Another wooden lady was stationed at the door to Nan's apartment. Her blue satin jacket, trimmed in beads and sequins and worn over wide-legged cream-colored silk pajama trousers, had been Fiona's costume, visitors learned from a card near the bidding box, worn to a policeman's ball to which she was escorted by Bullet Tolson.

Nan was the only one of the ladies not dressed by Fiona. She wore instead a long-sleeved crepe gown in a large sunflower print. To Pea, she was a masterpiece to rival her equally colorful paintings which, along with her seascapes, took up every bit of available wall space in her apartment. Each was assigned a number to facilitate the silent bidding. Offered for sale on the kitchen counter was an assortment of Nan's baked goods. From the looks of the money accumulating in a box nearby, and the crush of visitors admiring her work, Nan was a huge success.

"Like my dress, Pea?" she said, twirling on dangerous looking high-heeled slippers. "The editor of *Large and Luscious* Magazine gave it to me. She wants me to pose for the cover of an issue called *Dare to Wear Big Prints*."

Pea nodded his approval and accepted a fudge brownie before heading back to the foyer. He didn't want to miss the look on Lacy's face. He made it just in time to greet Mitch Sanders, who came in, winked at Lacy, shook Pea's hand, and said, "It's all arranged."

"What's all arranged?" Lacy said.

"You'll see," Pea smiled. "In good time." He turned back to Mitch. "And the press?"

"Couldn't beat them off with a stick."

"The press?" Lacy said. "I couldn't get a single reporter to commit."

Ignoring her, Pea handed Mitch a ticket, waving away his money.

"Thanks, Old Boy," Mitch said. "I'll just pay my respects to Fiona and then let myself out the back."

"Okay, Pea," Lacy said. "What's going on? I've a right to know."

"Yes, you do," he said, "and you shall." For once he was one step ahead of her and he enjoyed it immensely.

Outside, several reporters and photographers had gathered on the sidewalk in front of the awning. Pea drew Lacy to a vantage point inside the door just as a large man approached the entrance, then turned to face the reporters.

"Why that's Walker Knolls," Lacy said. "That awful zoning commission person. I just know Bertie's behind this. He's going to ruin the evening, isn't he? He could at least let Nan and the others have this one night."

Pea was touched that her first thought was for his ladies. It made him a little sorry for keeping her in the dark. "Quiet," he said. "Listen."

They didn't have to strain to hear, for someone had handed Walker Knolls a mike. "Good evening, Folks. It's an honor to be here and it's gratifying to see a good turnout for a worthy cause," he said.

"What does he mean, 'worthy cause'?" Lacy asked.

"Unfortunately," Knolls was saying, "it's not in my power to promise the lovely ladies who dwell here their beloved home will not be demolished, but I'm pleased to have removed at least one obstacle to its survival. This morning, the zoning commission called a special meeting and voted down the owner's request for a change in zoning. This venerable edifice has graced this city for too long to see it fall heir to the greed some mistake for progress."

"Did I hear him right?" Lacy said. "He and Bertie go way back. I took it for granted he'd be bought off."

"How about a shot with the doorman?" a photographer called out.

Walker Knolls chuckled and sidled up to the uniformed mannequin. "I recall the day when no one got in or out without the say-so of this gentleman."

"Mr. Knolls," a reporter said, "Didn't you just last week refer to Hobarth Manor as an impediment to progress? And didn't you say the community would be better served with a structure that afforded more housing?"

"Housing, yes." Knolls said. "A crucial issue, especially for the elderly, and one I will continue to address throughout my campaign for the legislature. Now I see we're blocking the entrance. May I lead the way inside? I invite you all to take part in the festivities."

"Something's going on," Lacy said. "This is too good to be true. And he acts as if he arranged the whole evening."

"No, no more questions," Knolls was saying. "This evening is not about me, after all. Allow me to give you these cards with the number of my campaign headquarters. You may find the answers to all your questions there."

"Answers, maybe," Lacy said. "But how about the questions? How did you do this, Pea? What brought him over to our side? That is, if he really has had a change of heart."

Pea grinned. "Let's just say Maizie was more right than she knew when she said we should look where the bodies are buried. Sure wish she was here to see this." With that, he left Lacy to the business of waiting on Walker Knolls as he made a great show of purchasing a ticket, then posing for a photograph of himself kissing the hand of the mannequin wearing Bullet Tolson's favorite hat.

He also kissed the gloved hand of the silent lady posed at the top of the stairs. She was dressed in a red satin off the shoulder gown with a shirred waist held together in front with a cluster of gardenias. A silver fox wrap hung over one arm. Having begun, the commissioner seemed to feel obligated to pay his respects to all the vintage-clad mannequins, including the three posed with their backs turned, at the Venetian window. The green gown in the center was cut deep in back with a large purple bow and ribbon reaching to the hemline. On the right, mulberry and emerald ribbons were twisted together on the black velvet over the low neckline and in a column down the spine, the colors parting at the hem to trim the right side in mulberry, the left in emerald. And the silver lamé gown had strings of pearl beads swinging down the back. The visiting politician placed a bid in the box for the beribboned black velvet.

"How much did you bid, Sir?" asked a reporter.

"Well now, we do have a secret ballot in this great country," he said, "but I'm betting on my wife wearing this to the next inaugural ball."

By this time, Hobarth Manor was crowded with guests taking advantage of the opportunity to bid, sample, donate, or mourn the passing of Maizie, who was quickly becoming a local folk hero, or simply to admire the uniqueness of the building and its inhabitants.

Walker Knolls stopped outside Sulie's apartment to appreciate a mannequin wearing a fitted red wool coat trimmed in fur, black leather gauntlet gloves, and a red felt hat with a shovel-fronted brim. He picked up the tastefully lettered card, but hastily returned it after reading Fiona had worn this costume at Bullet Tolson's trial.

Inside, the politician enjoyed a sampling of turtle soup before taking advantage of a photo-op with the famous cook. As a child, he told her, his family had often held family celebrations at the Snapper Stew, and yes, he did recall her husband. To all appearances, he was genuinely touched by the encounter.

He posed also with Carlotta at her piano, but he avoided altogether *Fiona's Closet.*

Although no one could later positively swear to it, when the strains of Mozart gave way to Carlotta's original composition, the light in Hobarth Manor took on sepia tones, giving the atmosphere the quality of a dreamscape. Some of the guests filing through Nan's apartment experienced nostalgic longings for childhood vacations at the sea. Others felt their imaginations touched with brilliant colors and movement and were filled with unexpressed longings. All were inspired to bid on one or more of her paintings.

The most popular painting was an abstract of Hobarth Manor, which showed the caryatids giving off a heavenly light and portraits of the ladies in various positions: Maizie dancing about on the lawn with a *Save Hobarth Manor* sign. Sulie and Fiona and Carlotta on the roof, arms outstretched to Nan as she flew out of the skylight. Pea in his blue suit flying alongside, holding her hand. The building itself was supported by a giant turtle.

For just a moment, a damp, green smell washed over Sulie's apartment, and she glanced uneasily toward the glass case holding the oak stick. Fiona lost her train of thought in the middle of a story. Lacy threw off her hat with the wax flowers and shook out her hair, and Nan gazed inward at her next painting.

Carlotta's notes became brighter and took on a peculiar rhythm suggesting waves splashing on a distant shore. All these ephemeral impressions were fleeting, yet timeless, as Carlotta returned again and again to various motifs. Reporters wandering through Nan's gallery were inspired to record rhapsodic impressions in their notebooks.

Strangest of all, the mannequins seemed to shift in a dance without measurable movement. Walker Knolls felt a tap on his shoulder and glanced around uneasily. It was only Bullet Tolson's favorite bracelet jangling on a lifeless wrist, but for a moment it looked like a golden handcuff. He hurriedly placed a generous bid on a more traditional rendering of Hobarth Manor, a simple watercolor of only the building. For the wall of his campaign office, he told a reporter. To remind him to always see to the needs of the less powerful in society. Then he took his leave.

The evening had been a resounding success, and by all reports, Leonardo was delicious.

Epilogue

As it turned out, the photo of two men shaking hands that Pea had observed on the wall, when he'd gone to enquire about his missing paycheck, was of Lacy's husband and Walker Knolls (formerly known as 'Sneezy' during his career in the mob.) A reporter got wind of some shady deals the two were involved in. Although Walker Knolls slipped through the prosecutor's net, Lacy's husband did not. As a result, she won control of her father's trust fund and subsequently gained possession of Hobarth Manor in the divorce settlement. It is now known as the Hobarth Manor Retirement Villa for Ladies. It's funded in part through the Maizie Dillard Foundation and partly through special legislation pushed through by Senator Knolls.

All the apartments are now filled, with a waiting list, for word is out that Hobarth manor is not a retirement home so much as a life school. Three days a week, Nan teaches art. And on Saturday mornings she conducts a weight loss class, incorporating her version of art therapy. *Love your Fat to Death* she calls it. Her philosophy is simple: refocus; take your mind off your waistline; find something you love to do.

Sulie holds classes in cooking, regularly attended by apprentices of the best chefs in the city. Carlotta gives piano lessons and has established a women's chorus, which performs throughout the community. Fiona operates a boutique, held in partnership with her old friend Mitch Sanders, a regular visitor at Hobarth Manor. She takes time out to provide makeovers for Nan's Saturday morning students.

But most of those developments occurred after Pea and Lacy were married at their rock in the park. Pea is now part owner of Hobarth Manor. He continues to take care of the building, and the ladies take care of him.

www.ingramcontent.com/pod-product-compliance
Lightning Source LLC
Chambersburg PA
CBHW052145070526
44585CB00017B/1982